CONTENTS OF PROJECT PREPARATION HANDBOOK

VOLUME 1: GUIDELINES

Table of Contents

WORLD BANK TECHNICAL PAPER NUMBER 12

Water Supply and Sanitation Project Preparation Handbook

Volume 1: Guidelines

Brian Grover

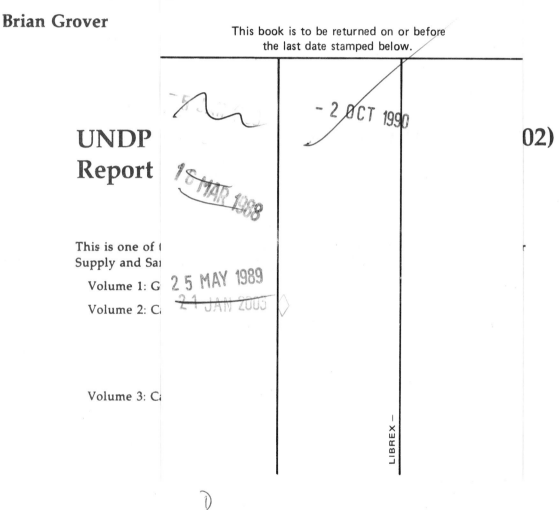

UNDP (02)

Report

This is one of
Supply and Sa

Volume 1: G

Volume 2: C

Volume 3: C

The World Bank
Washington, D.C., U.S.A.

This is a document published informally by the World Bank. In order that the information contained in it can be presented with the least possible delay, the typescript has not been prepared in accordance with the procedures appropriate to formal printed texts, and the World Bank accepts no responsibility for errors. The publication is supplied at a token charge to defray part of the cost of manufacture and distribution.

The views and interpretations in this document are those of the author(s) and should not be attributed to the World Bank, to its affiliated organizations, or to any individual acting on their behalf. Any maps used have been prepared solely for the convenience of the readers; the denominations used and the boundaries shown do not imply, on the part of the World Bank and its affiliates, any judgment on the legal status of any territory or any endorsement or acceptance of such boundaries.

The full range of the World Bank publications is described in the *Catalog of World Bank Publications*. The *Catalog* is updated annually; the most recent edition is available without charge from the Publications Distribution Unit of the Bank in Washington or from the European Office of the Bank, 66, avenue d'Iéna, 75116 Paris, France.

Library of Congress Cataloging in Publication Data

Grover, Brian, 1939–
    Water supply and sanitation project preparation handbook.
    (World Bank technical paper no. 12-14)
    Vol. 2-3: by Brian Grover, Nicholas Burnett and Michael McGarry.
    "A contribution to the International Drinking Water Supply and Sanitation Decade by the World Bank and the United Nations Development Programme under the auspices of the I.D.W.S.S.D. Steering Committee."
    Bibliography: p.
    Contents: v. 1. Guidelines — v. 2. Case studies: identification report for Port City, immediate improvement project for Port City, pre-feasibility report for Farmville, pre-feasibility report for Port City — v. 3. Case study: feasibility report for Port City.
    1. Sanitary engineering—Developing countries—Handbooks, manuals, etc. 2. Water-supply engineering—Developing countries—Handbooks, manuals, etc. I. Burnett, Nicholas. II. McGarry, Michael. III. World Bank. IV. United Nations Development Programme. V. Title. VI. Series.
TD153.G75 1983   363.6'1'091724   83-14590
ISBN 0-8213-0230-2 (pbk.: v. 1.)
ISBN 0-8213-0231-0 (pbk.: v. 2.)
ISBN 0-8213-0232-9 (pbk.: v. 3.)

Page

FOREWORD

Close to three billion people in the developing countries will need improved water supply and sanitation services by 1990. This is the ambitious goal of the International Drinking Water Supply and Sanitation Decade (IDWSSD).

Among the major impediments to meeting this goal are a scarcity of expertise for planning good projects and the lack of globally accepted project preparation standards. The limited human and financial resources in developing countries can be used more efficiently if water and sanitation projects are initially prepared to standards meeting requirements of approving authorities and financing agencies.

The Steering Committee of United Nations Agencies involved in promoting the Decade was urged by developing country representatives to set out, and make uniform to the extent practicable, the information requirements of the agencies which provide financial assistance for water supply and sanitation projects. At the request of this Steering Committee, the World Bank commissioned the development of this Project Preparation Handbook by three consultants, as part of the Bank-executed United Nations Development Programme (UNDP) Project "Information and Training for Low Cost Water Supply and Sanitation".

The Handbook consists of a set of Guidelines, setting out the information requirements, and accompanying Case Studies which illustrate how the Guidelines might be followed for specific projects. The Guidelines and Case Studies are mainly addressed to proponents of water supply and sanitation projects in the developing countries. They explain the process of project development from the perspective of the agencies which might be asked to provide financial assistance. Guidelines are suggested and illustrated for the reports expected on completion of three successive stages of pre-investment planning for specific projects: identification, pre-feasibility and feasibility. In addition a Guideline is provided for preparing a program of rural water supply and sanitation.

Guidelines cannot be a substitute for professional judgement. They provide guidance, suggest approaches and methods of evaluation, and must be sufficiently comprehensive to be useful in many situations, covering projects of various complexities. They must be used flexibly. The extent to which specific suggestions are followed, and in what detail, must be left to the professional judgement of the planner. As a consequence, the selection of staff responsible for project preparation, and local and foreign consultants to assist them, if necessary, is the most important step an agency takes in project development.

Flexibility in the application of the Guidelines has been a major consideration in their preparation. The three project Guidelines of Volume 1 do not distinguish between urban, semi-urban or rural projects because the principles and methods elaborated, properly applied, will result in the most cost effective project, regardless of location or size. The final Guideline, however, is specially designed for a rural program, involving a number of sub-projects for water supply and sanitation.

Because urban and semi-urban projects provide better opportunities for demonstrating the full scope of the Guidelines, urban projects have been selected for the Case Studies of Volumes 2 and 3. Even within that framework, the Case Studies demonstrate different levels of preparation, reflecting projects of different complexities: a simple project for a small town; an immediate improvement program and a large and complex project for a major city.

Many individuals in the bilateral and multilateral agencies and other organizations named in the following list have reviewed the Guidelines and, in most cases, the Case Studies. Their thoughtful comments, all of which are gratefully acknowledged, led to substantial revisions and improvements to the Handbook. Listing these reviewers does not imply in any sense that these documents reflect all their comments or represent the official policies of their institutions. Given the variety of institutional objectives, it would be impossible, indeed, undesirable, to have one single, rigid standard. What the authors have attempted to do is to present a methodology and approach which will result in a plan for a quality project whatever its complexity. Project proponents and development agencies should together decide on the degree of detail that any specific project requires. In this sense, hopefully, the documents do represent a standard acceptable to many institutions. The IDWSSD Donor Catalogue is a first source of information about the particular requirements of various international development agencies.

This Handbook will remain valuable only as long as it remains up to date. We therefore anticipate future revisions to reflect new developments and experience gained in the use of the documents. Similarly, the addition of other Case Studies might be helpful. We would appreciate receiving comments and suggestions for incorporation in future volumes. Users of the Handbook are encouraged to send comments derived from its practical application to the address below.

S. Arlosoroff,
Chief, Applied Research
and Technology Division,
Water Supply and Urban
Development Department,
The World Bank

John M. Kalbermatten
Senior Adviser,
Water Supply and Urban
Development Department,
The World Bank

November 1983

ACKNOWLEDGEMENTS

This Handbook is a product of the World Bank-executed UNDP Project INT/82/002 "INFORMATION AND TRAINING FOR LOW COST WATER SUPPLY AND SANITATION" . Other project outputs which will become available during 1984 are films, audio-visual training modules, manuals, guidelines and visual learning kits. A Project Brochure describing objectives and target audiences as well as the format and content of the material to be produced is available from the Applied Research and Technology Division, Water Supply and Urban Development Department (WUD), World Bank, 1818 H Street, N. W., Washington, D. C. 20433, U.S.A.

Project INT/82/002 was initiated with financial support from the Canadian International Development Agency (CIDA), the National Film Board of Canada (NFB), the United Nations Center for Human Settlements (UNCHS), the United Nations Development Programme (UNDP), and the World Bank. Subsequently, the United Nations Children's Fund (UNICEF), the Finnish International Development Agency (FINNIDA), the Gesellschaft fur Technische Zusammenarbeit (GTZ) of the Federal Republic of Germany and the Directorate of Development Cooperation of Switzerland provided financial assistance.

In addition to INT/82/002, the following UNDP projects executed by the World Bank contributed to this Handbook: the Regional Offices for the Preparation of Water and Sanitation Projects in Asia (RAS/81/001) and in Africa (RAF/82/004), the Field Testing and Technological Development of Rural Water Supply Handpumps Project (INT/81/026) and the Research and Development in Integrated Resource Recovery Project (GLO/80/004).

Finally, we wish to express our gratitude to the authors of the Handbook, Brian Grover, Nicholas Burnett and Michael McGarry, who deserve credit for a difficult job well done, and to the collaborators whose contributions have greatly improved these documents: Mr. Leo Lawson, Director of Engineering of the National Water Commission of Jamaica; Mr. John Sipper, Economic Editor, Asian Development Bank; and Mr. Joseph Freedman, Rural Water and Sanitation Adviser of the World Bank's Water Supply and Urban Development Department.

The support of all these agencies, projects and individuals is gratefully acknowledged.

LIST OF REVIEWERS

The following organizations have reviewed one or more volumes of the Project Preparation Handbook. Their comments have greatly contributed to the value of these documents and are hereby gratefully acknowledged by the International Drinking Water Supply and Sanitation Decade Steering Committee, the World Bank, and the authors. The list of reviewers includes those who commented on the initial version of the guidelines (Volume 1) beginning early in 1981. It is possible, therefore, that some of the individuals named no longer hold the positions described.

Organization	Individuals
Asian Development Bank	David A. Howarth Manager Water Supply Division John Sipper Economic Editor
Canadian International Development Agency	Walter I. Marshall Chief Water Sector Infrastructure Division Resources Branch
Danish International Development Agency	Birte Poulsen Head of Section
Food and Agriculture Organization of the United Nations	T.H. Mather Senior Officer Water Resources, Development and Management Service Land and Water Development Division
Instituto Nacional de Fomento Municipal Colombia	Nelson Amaya Director General
International Development Research Centre Canada	Donald S. Sharp Associate Director Water Supply and Sanitation Health Sciences Division
International Reference Centre for Community Water Supply and Sanitation The Netherlands	J.M.G. Van Damme Director T.K. Tjiook Programme Officer

Organization	Individuals
London School of Hygiene and Tropical Medicine	Richard Feachem Senior Lecturer in Tropical Public Health Engineering
Ministry for Foreign Affairs of Finland	Jorma Paukku Chief of Section Department of International Development Co-operation
Ministry of Housing and Urban Development India	P.K. Chatterjee Adviser Central Public Health and Environmental Engineering Office
Ministry of Works and Development New Zealand	C.F. Candy Investigation Engineer (Development and Aid Coordinator)
Nairobi City Commission Kenya	Peter K. Karimi Deputy General Manager Water and Sewerage Department
National Water Commission Jamaica	Leo Lawson Director of Engineering
National Water Council United Kingdom	David J. Kinnersley Senior Economic Adviser
Norwegian Agency for International Development	Kjell Storløkken Chief Building and Construction Division
Overseas Development Administration United Kingdom	B.M.U. Bennell Principal Engineering Adviser M.B. Grieveson Principal Engineering Adviser
Reid Crowther & Partners Limited Canada and Jamaica	Heinz K. Unger Project Engineer
Swedish International Development Agency	Leif Rosenhall Head Water Section

Organization	Individuals
United Nations Centre for Human Settlements	Nicholas Houghton Chief Technical Adviser BCCI Orangi Rehabilitation Pilot Project Pakistan
United Nations Children's Fund	Martin Beyer Senior Policy Specialist
United Nations Department of Technical Cooperation for Development	Enzo Fano Deputy Director Water Resources Branch Division of Natural Resources and Energy
United Nations Development Programme	Michael Potashnik Senior Program Officer Division of Global and Inter Regional Projects Consultant: Mary Elmendorf
United Nations Environment Programme	Peter S. Thatcher Assistant Secretary-General
United Nations International Research and Training Institute for the Advancement of Women	Dunja Pastizzi-Ferencic Director
United States Agency for International Development	F.E. McJunkin Chief Community Water Supply and Sanitation Division Office of Health Bureau of Science and Technology
R.L. Walker & Partners Ltd. Canada	James B. Kirch Director
World Bank/UNDP Demonstration Projects in Low-cost Water Supply and Sanitation	Richard Middleton Manager Staff and Consultants: R.A. Boydell, Paul V. Hébert, Duncan D. Mara, Heli Perret, A.K. Roy, and Augusto Sergio Pinto Guimaraes

Organization	Individuals
World Bank/UNDP Water Supply and Sanitation Project Preparation Unit for Africa	Tauno Skytta Investment Projects Adviser
World Bank	David Cook Engineering Adviser Urban Development Department Joseph Freedman Water and Wastes Adviser Transportation and Water Department Francis J. Lethem Technical Cooperation Adviser Projects Advisory Staff M.S. Nanjundiah Financial Adviser Transportation and Water Department Gloria Scott Adviser on Women in Development Projects Advisory Staff Alain Thys Chief Water Supply & Sewerage Division Europe, Middle East and North Africa Regional Office Staff: Bill Barker, Art Bruestle, John Courtney, Fred Golladay, Al Heron, David Jones, Mel Loewen, Robert MacWilliam, John Nebiker, John Pettigrew, Carlo Rietveld, and Steve Serdahely

World Health Organization
  (WHO)
    Switzerland
	Somnuek Unakul
	Manager
	Environmental Health Technology and
	  Support
	Division of Environmental Health
	
	Staff:
	Martin Jackson, Mahmood Suleiman,
	G. Schultzberg, and A. Vogel

Organization	Individuals
WHO Regional Office for Africa	Léo Roy Director Environmental Health Protection
WHO Regional Office for South East Asia	D.V. Subrahmanyam Regional Adviser on Environmental Health Consultant: V.K. Nayar
WHO Regional Office for the Americas (Pan American Health Organization)	Guillermo H. Dávila Acting Coordinator Environmental Health Program

PREFACE TO THE GUIDELINES

Developing countries supply the bulk of investment funds needed to improve their water supply and sanitation services, complemented by assistance from international sources. Sector staff in these countries need to find ways to prepare projects as efficiently as possible, regardless of the sources of finance. This Handbook has been prepared to assist these efforts.

The Guidelines presented in Volume 1 of this Handbook foresee three levels of project preparation to satisfy the information needs of different agencies, for projects of variable complexities. Project identification provides minimal information, sufficient to determine how a project fits into a development or assistance program and to attract financial support. The pre-feasibility stage provides considerably more information which permits the selection of preferred alternatives and may suffice for investment decisions about relatively simple projects. The feasibility stage, finally, provides the full justification necessary for complex and large projects. Reports for the various stages of project preparation are illustrated by means of Case Studies in Volumes 2 and 3 of the Handbook.

The preparation of a program of sub-projects for water supply and sanitation in rural communities normally proceeds somewhat differently than for any single project. Readers concerned exclusively with rural programs may accordingly be more interested in the fourth Guideline in this volume, which explains how such a program can be prepared. This rural guideline has been written by John Kalbermatten, incorporating much information previously assembled by Joseph Freedman of the World Bank.

Those requiring further information concerning project preparation are referred to the Case Studies for examples of typical reports; to the bibliography in this volume for reference material; and to more experienced planners in their own country or to project officers from bilateral and international development agencies, who can provide advice and guidance.

The development of these Guidelines has been a major task which could not have been completed without the assistance and cooperation which many people have so willingly provided. In addition to the many individuals who have reviewed the earlier drafts, the author also wishes to acknowledge help from staff members in several departments in the World Bank; from colleagues in the author's consulting firm; and particularly from Nicholas Burnett and Michael McGarry, who collaborated to produce the Case Studies of Volumes 2 and 3. Thanks to all.

Ottawa
June, 1983

Brian Grover

A. INTRODUCTION

Purpose and Scope of these Guidelines

1.   These Guidelines provide a practical basis for preparing projects in the water supply and sanitation sector in developing countries. Their main purpose is to make the process of project preparation easier by clarifying and, to the extent possible, standardizing the type of information that should appear in all project preparation reports. Their scope is deliberately broad and covers general concepts, issues and principles which apply to water supply and sanitation projects in both rural and urban areas.

2.   These Guidelines are mainly for the use of planners, engineers, community development, and public health specialists in developing countries and their consultants who prepare projects which require financial assistance from external sources. They are aimed at senior professionals who are responsible for sector planning and who must translate general principles of water supply and sanitation into practical procedures and realistic projects.

3.   The way in which projects are prepared for the consideration of bilateral and multilateral agencies should not be very different from the way in which projects are prepared for financing by local sources. As such, methods and Guidelines for project preparation and evaluation suggested in this Handbook are valid regardless of the sources of finance and should serve as the basis for preparing water supply and sanitation projects no matter where the financing comes from.

4.   Although these Guidelines may appear too detailed and demand too much information, such detail is considered necessary and useful to the planner of major, complex projects. However, the amount of information required in a project preparation report remains a matter of professional judgment and agreement with the agency that intends to help finance the project.

5.   These Guidelines provide the framework for preparing any project in the sector and suggest different levels of project preparation. They outline what information is expected in project identification, pre-feasibility and feasibility reports. The Guidelines also explain how the normal stages of project preparation which a developing country follows in preparing a project for internal approval are coordinated with the procedures followed by external agencies in appraising a project.

6.   The first three Guidelines mainly deal with the preparation of a single project, with less emphasis on the preparation of sector programs (even though sector program preparation is basically the sum total of pre-investment planning activities for a series of individual

However, the fourth Guideline provides advice on the preparation of water supply and sanitation improvements for a number of rural communities. This program approach, involving several sub-projects, incorporates and simplifies the process involved in preparing individual projects.

7.   Since no Guidelines can anticipate all possible questions associated with preparing water supply and sanitation sector projects, these should be used only as a guide and not an inflexible set of rules. It is likely that the actual process of preparing any specific project could result in reports which deviate considerably from those suggested in these general Guidelines[1]/. Project planners are encouraged to follow the general framework outlined herein but to apply their judgement in determining exactly how any particular project should proceed. Guidance should be obtained at the outset from the agencies expected to help finance the project and from national authorities with previous experience in preparing projects for these agencies.

8.   The presentation of the information in each report can be varied to suit the intended audience. Background information, for example, can often be presented in annexes with the main text concentrating on the basic logic and conclusions. Examples of alternative means of presenting information are provided in the Case Studies.

Project Objectives and Components

9.   In this Handbook:

-- The word project refers to the entire set of actions taken to meet specific objectives. This involves the planning, design, construction and initial operation of physical facilities plus the provision of all other inputs needed to meet the objectives of the project.

-- The components are constituent parts of a project necessary to achieve its objectives. These components can be physical facilities or supporting activities. Physical facilities are sometimes referred to in other publications as "hardware" and supporting activities as "software".

1/   The Case Studies provided in Volumes 2 and 3 of this Handbook do not conform precisely to the report formats suggested in the Guidelines.

— The objectives should be broadly specified by the impact they will have on people in the project area and, more narrowly, by the physical, financial and institutional accomplishments which are to be achieved.

10.   In some cases, a project for which financial assistance is being sought cannot achieve its objectives unless other inputs, often from other sectors, are provided. For example, improvements in living standards and public health in a community may be impossible to achieve unless hygiene education is provided and sanitation improvements are made concurrently with a water supply project.

11.   A water supply project, for example, could be defined as a set of physical components (dams, treatment plants, pipelines, etc.) and a set of supporting activities (staff training, management assistance, etc.). Essential complementary inputs (such as primary health care centres or sanitation improvements) would also have to be defined, planned and incorporated into an overall program, which then might be carried out by one or more agencies not directly responsible for the water supply project.

12.   The definition and refinement of project objectives and project components is a process which may need to continue throughout project preparation and implementation. Different agencies may be required at different stages of project implementation.

Stages in Project Development

13.   All projects go through a series of distinct stages between the initial idea and the time when the project is completed. These Guidelines are intended to assist those involved in the planning of projects but there is merit in briefly examining such planning activities in the context of other stages in the development of the project. The various stages are shown on Figure 1, and can be summarized as follows:

— Identification   and   Preparation   comprise   the pre-investment   planning   stages   which   are   discussed subsequently;

— Approval is the stage where decision makers, including financiers, determine whether or not the project will be transformed from an idea into reality;

— Implementation is the stage when detailed designs are completed and the project facilities are built and commissioned. Supporting activities such as staff training are also underway;

FIGURE 1

DEVELOPMENT STAGES FOR WATER SUPPLY AND SANITATION PROJECTS

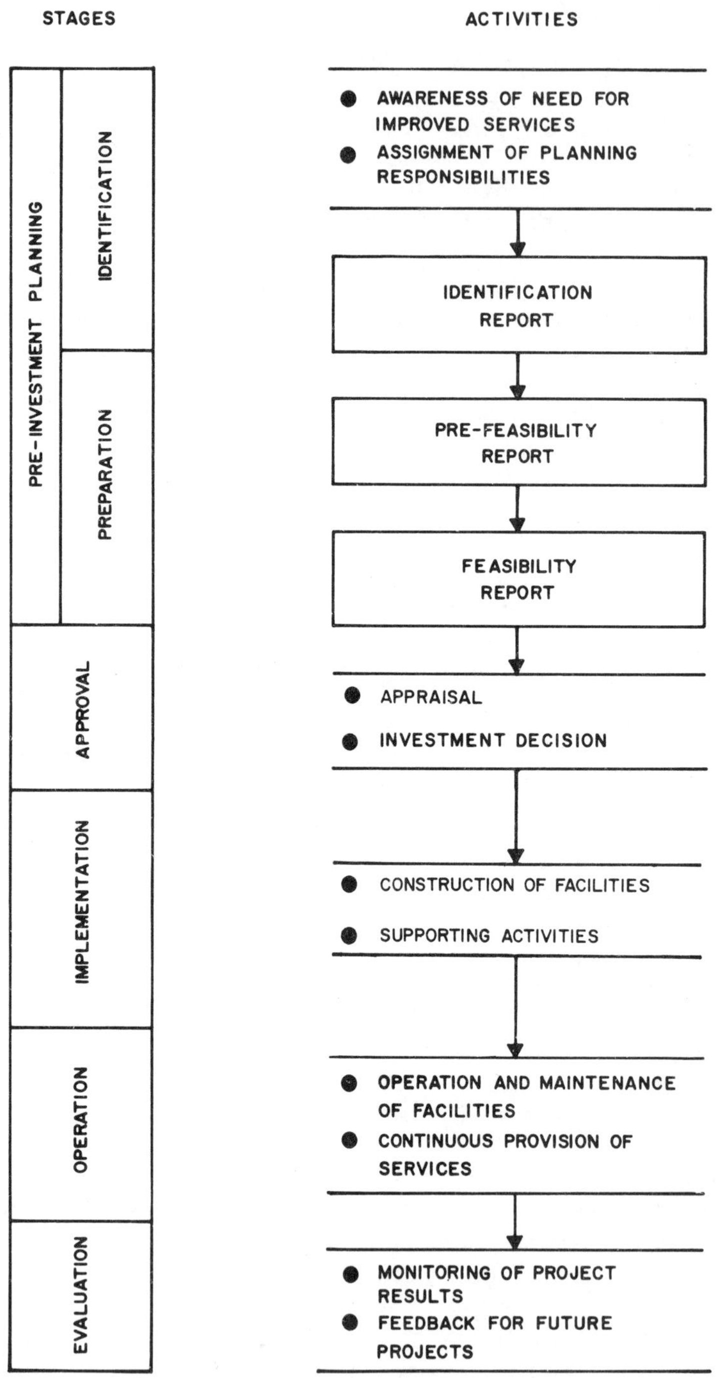

STAGES   ACTIVITIES

PRE-INVESTMENT PLANNING

- IDENTIFICATION
- PREPARATION

APPROVAL

IMPLEMENTATION

OPERATION

EVALUATION

Activities:

- AWARENESS OF NEED FOR IMPROVED SERVICES
- ASSIGNMENT OF PLANNING RESPONSIBILITIES

IDENTIFICATION REPORT

PRE-FEASIBILITY REPORT

FEASIBILITY REPORT

- APPRAISAL
- INVESTMENT DECISION

- CONSTRUCTION OF FACILITIES
- SUPPORTING ACTIVITIES

- OPERATION AND MAINTENANCE OF FACILITIES
- CONTINUOUS PROVISION OF SERVICES

- MONITORING OF PROJECT RESULTS
- FEEDBACK FOR FUTURE PROJECTS

-- <u>Operation</u> is when the project facilities are integrated with the existing system to provide improved services;

-- <u>Evaluation</u>, the final stage, determines what lessons have been learned so that future projects can be improved accordingly.

14.   It is important that both the agency proposing the project and the potential source of finance have a common frame of reference when discussing the various activities involved in project development. Requirements of financing agencies vary with project size and complexity and they should therefore be consulted to determine what degree of preparation is required for a specific project. Annex 1 is a reprint of a World Bank paper which describes project preparation and the project cycle from a multilateral agency's point of view and reviews, in particular, such an agency's participation in the process. The paper is reproduced here not because it reflects World Bank requirements (it may not, because they continue to evolve) but because it is the best description of the process known to the authors.

Pre-Investment Planning Activities

15.   The pre-investment planning activities covering the first two stages in Figure 1 are the main subject to these Guidelines. The reports produced during the identification and preparation stages are summarized as follows:

Identification

-- The project identification report provides an overview of the existing water supply and sanitation systems, the need for the project, and a brief description of the indicated project and its alternatives and order-of-magnitude costs.

-- At this stage the planner explains the project and its priority within the context of national and regional development plans for the sector.

-- Steps to complete the preparation of the project are defined.

This stage is basically a "desk study", relying primarily on existing information. It does not involve extensive site investigations but should be firmly based on the conditions in the project area. From this study a brief report is prepared which sets in motion the more detailed phases of project preparation, assuming that the necessary approval has been obtained following submission and review of the Identification Report. Private voluntary organizations who participate in project implementation with their own staff, and bilateral and other development agencies doing the same, generally require less detailed preparation. They may well provide technical assistance and funding on the basis of an identification report, especially in the case of rural water supply and sanitation, where standard designs are used, provided institutional arrangements are satisfactory.

Pre-feasibility

-- The pre-feasibility report analyzes past, present and future demand for services. It also examines existing systems, the degree to which these systems meet all demands in the project area, and the possible need to rehabilitate them.

-- This report presents a preliminary screening and ranking of alternative projects and their staging and eliminates those which are technically and economically inferior or culturally unacceptable.

-- Based on limited fieldwork (to support basic analysis) the pre-feasibility report contains information which should result in a strategic plan for:

  o the staged development of facilities to meet the long term needs for services; and

  o the selection of one or two superior projects which warrant more detailed planning to confirm their feasibility for possible implementation in the near term.

-- At this stage initial consideration is given to institutional arrangements and financial implications for project implementation, and community selection and design criteria for multicommunity (urban-rural) projects are determined. Other supporting activities such as hygiene education and staff training are also considered.

The pre-feasibility report, whose principal purpose is to determine the preferred project to be evaluated in the feasibility study, is based on limited data supported by surveys to obtain preliminary estimates of critical information. A pre-feasibility report may be sufficient to obtain financial support for small- and medium-size, less complex projects or for sub-projects in a sector program when agencies have previously agreed on sub-project selection and design criteria.

Feasibility

-- The feasibility report confirms the rationale for selecting the preferred project.

-- It provides preliminary designs and cost estimates for this project, based on considerable data gathering and analysis, with input from ultimate users. It also defines and costs supporting activities.

-- At this stage the planner gives detailed consideration to institutional arrangements (both at agency and community level), the subsequent operation and maintenance of facilities, and financial aspects.

-- This study considers all probable impacts and concludes whether the project is technically and institutionally feasible, financially viable, socio-culturally acceptable and economically justified.

The feasibility report for large and complex projects normally forms the basis for the appraisal report and investment decision by financing agencies, after which implementation could proceed without delay. However, some agencies require that detailed designs be completed before financing can be approved. Any agency from which finance is sought should be given an opportunity to review the feasibility report before design work is undertaken.

16. Major projects will normally proceed through these three stages. Each stage should be part of a screening process whereby alternative projects are more carefully reviewed until a reduced number of superior options remain. Since this screening process will cause certain alternatives to be dropped at each stage, there should be a greater number of potential projects being considered in the earlier stages of the preparation process than at the feasibility stage. The cost involved in the preliminary analysis and screening of projects which are later dropped or deferred is usually much lower than the cost of proceeding with a less-than-optimal project.

17. Agencies considering projects serving small towns and rural communities may not require the detailed analysis normally provided at the feasibility stage prior to reaching their investment decision. Smaller and less complex projects which form part of a sector program can be designed during the implementation process, based on agreed upon community selection and project design criteria. In such cases the investment decision could be made on the basis of a pre-feasibility study which resulted in suitable selection and design criteria for project implementation. The Case Studies of Volume 2 provide examples of such pre-feasibility studies.

18.   These Guidelines coordinate the usual stages of project preparation which a developing country follows to obtain funding from external agencies. The basic principle to remember is that decision points exist between each stage in the development of a project. The decision which must be made at each new stage of project preparation is whether to proceed to the next planning stage and, in doing so, commit more human and financial resources to the project. In other words, resources should not be committed to a feasibility report (the most costly stage) unless good prospects exist in the near term for implementing the project. Local communities should be included in the decision-making process so that there is careful consideration of all implications.

19.   Whenever a developing country intends to seek external assistance to develop a project, communications between the project proponent and the external agency should begin as soon as possible. In this way, each side will have an early and clear understanding of what reports will be submitted at each stage of project preparation. These discussions will also ensure that the Guidelines presented in this Handbook can be modified for any particular project to take account of specific conditions.

20.   Early communications can have other benefits, including technical advice and assistance from agency staff and financial assistance to help meet the expenses associated with project preparation. Many external agencies provide grants or loans specifically for the preparation of projects, prior to any consideration of funding for implementation. Another possibility is to obtain project preparation funds through loans or grants for rehabilitation and engineering projects. The components of such a project could include the rehabilitation of existing facilities (treatment plants, distribution systems, meters, etc.), institutional improvements (accounting, billing and collection system, staff training and community involvement) and pre-feasibility and feasibility studies. A project identification report, suitably expanded to include information about rehabilitation and institutional needs, should normally be sufficient to obtain a funding decision for an engineering loan. Major rehabilitation projects would require more extensive justification.

21.   The end-product of each stage of pre-investment planning should be a report which clearly documents the status of the project for consideration by all relevant national authorities and the external agencies whose support is to be requested.[1]

_____

[1]   Sections B, C, and D of the Guidelines explain what kind of information is expected at the end of the project identification, pre-feasibility and feasibility stages. Section E provides a Guideline for preparing a program of various sub-projects for a rural area.

22.   Each report should contain a set of recommendations which, in some cases, will call for no further work to be carried out on one or more project alternatives because these alternatives have been determined not to be feasible.

23.   For attractive projects, the report should list the actions which must be taken for the project to proceed to the next stage. A timetable and a cost estimate should accompany each recommended action required for the next stage. Each report should also include a realistic schedule for all future stages of project development and allow sufficient time for the relevant organizations involved in:

-- review and approval of the completed report;

-- resolution of policy issues identified in the project;

-- providing funding for the next stage of project preparation;

-- mobilizing personnel (possibly consultants) for the next stage of project preparation;

-- data gathering, including interviews, participant observations, physical surveys, and site investigations;

-- issue and review of interim reports during the next stage;

-- completion of separate tasks in the following stage;

-- printing and distribution of reports;

-- review and reactions to recommendations for action.

Project Preparation for Sector Programs

24.   The Guidelines deal primarily with the preparation of any single project. For a small and relatively simple project, such as the provision of water supply and sanitation facilities for a small town or village, most external agencies would generally be satisfied having the kind of information provided by a pre-feasibility report as outlined in Section C. For large projects and projects that will be operated by revenue-producing authorities, external agencies generally require that a comprehensive feasibility report (such as the type outlined in Section D) be completed before project appraisal.

25.   The project proponent should confirm at the start of the project preparation process what information is required by the intended financing agency. Even if an external agency agrees to provide

financing on the basis of a pre-feasibility study as set out in Section C, detailed designs usually must be prepared before the project can actually be built. Thus, implementation cannot proceed immediately after the pre-feasibility stage.

26.   It is common for regional or national development agencies to improve sector services in many separate locations during the same period of time through a package of individual sub-projects referred to as a "sector program." Agencies which provide development finance are often willing to support such programs by providing financial assistance on a sector program basis.

27.   Before such assistance for a sector program can be agreed, external agencies generally require that three main conditions be met. These are:

-- a national or regional agency must exist that can competently plan and manage the development of each individual sub-project within a comprehensive program;

-- the criteria for determining priorities within the sector must be satisfactory so that the most important sub-projects are implemented first;

-- the national or regional agency must have proven experience in the preparation and execution of similar sub-projects in accordance with agreed upon standards and criteria.

28.   In those cases where a proponent expects to obtain external assistance to finance a sector program, the situation should be explained to the selected external agency at the outset so that program preparation can proceed according to a mutually agreeable process.

29.   Normally an external agency would expect the national agency responsible for the program to prepare each individual sub-project according to agreed principles, including possibly those outlined in this Handbook. In such cases, the decision to provide assistance could be agreed upon (assuming other conditions were met) if a specified number of sub-projects were prepared to the pre-feasibility level outlined in Section C of these Guidelines. A large part of the subsequent detailed planning and implementation of individual sub-projects in the sector program would be the responsibility of the national agency, with only limited involvement of the external agency.

30.   Water supply and sanitation improvements for rural communities are frequently planned and implemented as part of an overall program, comprising several and sometimes many sub-projects. A sector program may include both urban and rural sub-projects, while a rural program would usually consist only of villages and small towns in a rural area. Section E of this report provides further information and guidance

concerning the preparation of a rural water supply and sanitation program. The discussion on program planning and sub-project selection criteria in that section applies generally to sector programs in urban or in rural areas. However, sub-projects in an urban program would normally be prepared according to the standards outlined for specific projects in Guidelines B, C and D, while sub-projects in a rural program would be prepared according to the Guidelines of Section E.

Organization and Resources Needed

31.   The process of taking a water supply or sanitation project from a concept to the operational stage is most effective when there is a clear understanding of what must be done in each stage of the process by each participant. After the pre-investment planning has been completed with a suitable feasibility report, there are several intermediate stages prior to the project becoming operational and providing the desired services. Intermediate stages include:

-- project appraisal and negotiations;

-- project implementation:

    o design, construction and commissioning of facilities,

    o human resource development, hygiene education and related supporting activities.

32.   The organizational arrangements required to bring a project into operation are critical to the success of the pre-investment planning stage. Accordingly, careful consideration must be given to the roles and perspectives of all groups who are involved in approving, implementing and finally operating and maintaining the project. This organizational planning and involvement can often affect the basic design of the project so it needs to be taken account of in project preparation activities from the outset.

33.   The basic responsibility for project preparation may change at various stages. A central planning agency, for example, might manage the identification stage and then transfer responsibility for later stages of the project to an agency that is more oriented to engineering and management . Specific arrangements need to be agreed upon for each stage of project preparation.

34.   Two or more organizations may each have a role in one or more stages of project preparation. A combination of health, engineering and social development groups, for example, may need to collaborate to prepare a water supply and sanitation project. Even so, it is essential that a single entity be responsible for the overall management and coordination of each stage of project preparation.

35.   After it has been decided who will be responsible for each stage of project preparation, the scope of the work, the timetable to carry out the work, and the output required from each group involved should be written down and formally agreed. This should include community commitments as well as agency responsibilities.

36.   All groups whose input is needed to implement a project should be kept informed and have at least a consultative role in project preparation. Likewise, organizations expected to participate in the operational stage should be actively involved at the preparation and implementation stages.

37.   Pre-investment planning requires considerable judgment and is not a job for inexperienced people. It requires a multidisciplinary approach with input from planners with considerable training and practical experience. The range of skills needed to develop a water supply or sanitation project properly is wide and includes expertise in:

   -- demography;
   -- engineering;
   -- human behavior;
   -- institutional analysis;
   -- regional and urban development;
   -- communications;
   -- public health;
   -- financial analysis;
   -- economics;
   -- training and education;
   -- management.

38.   Interaction between these various project planners is essential throughout the preparation process. They need to work together, more or less continuously, and share ideas and information as the work proceeds. This is true for the various engineering planners (for example water supply and sanitation experts) and even more true of the necessary linkages between these engineers and planners and other disciplines.

39.   All participants involved in project preparation should be aware of their collective responsibility and their individual inputs. Those responsible for managing the various stages and producing the reports must ensure that frequent and effective communications (both formal and informal) take place between the groups involved in the project as the interactive process of project preparation proceeds, right from the beginning.

40.   Consultants, both local and international, often provide some of the needed expertise. But, to be most effective, consultants must receive clear and continuing guidance from managers responsible for project preparation and must work closely with people who have good experience in sector activities in the region.

41.   The development of local expertise should be an important goal of any government's national strategy for improving water supply and sanitation services. For this reason, planners should carefully review the country's human resources (in both the private and public sectors) before deciding what amount of external assistance is necessary to enable new projects to be planned and implemented efficiently.

42.   The inputs required increase at each stage of pre-investment project preparation. The project identification report, for example, should require only a small percentage of the time and effort needed for a comprehensive feasibility report. Thorough preparation of a project up to the implementation stage normally takes one to two years. The implementation of major projects may take several years.

43.   The total effort involved in completing the pre-investment stage of a project, so that work on the project can begin as soon as the sources of funding are assured, typically costs from two to five percent of the final cost of the completed project. Such "front-end expenditures" are usually well justified since comprehensive planning makes future implementation of the project easier and keeps the final costs down. Errors in project planning can be extremely expensive if they result in changes or delays in project implementation. Spending a few more man-months in properly preparing a project usually pays significant dividends in terms of minimum time and costs for project implementation.

44.   The task of managing the process of project preparation to ensure that it proceeds and concludes satisfactorily involves realistic scheduling and reliable estimates of required resources, plus constant monitoring, evaluation and feedback through regular progress reports. Once the project facilities are commissioned, project preparation and implementation should be evaluated so future activities can be improved. The actual operation and performance of the project should be monitored and evaluated at regular intervals so that appropriate remedial measures can be taken if necessary and improvements cna be made to existing and future projects.

B. GUIDELINE FOR PROJECT IDENTIFICATION REPORT

45.   A brief report is all that is needed to identify possible projects and begin pre-investment planning. At this stage there are four main goals which must be achieved. These are:

-- to explain the need for a project;

-- to draw attention to one or more alternative projects which merit priority support from the national government and external financing agencies;

-- to estimate the tentative cost of the project and place it into the proper planning and budgeting cycles;

-- to obtain authorization and financial resources needed to carry out the pre-feasibility and feasibility stages.

46.   The project identification report can be prepared reasonably quickly if the planner is familiar with the sector and the region and if a regional development plan and sector program are available. Where there is considerable information already available and some analysis has already been carried out, such a knowledgeable planner should be able to produce the report chiefly on the basis of a "desk study". It is essential, however, that the project area and site be inspected to ensure that existing background information is realistic and that future developments are unlikely to provide any surprises to project planners. If there is little existing data and analysis, some crude estimates of necessary facilities and their costs will have to be made. The following check-list shows the kind of information which should be included in a project identification report:

-- provide a map showing the project area and define the intended beneficiaries;

-- explain how the proposed project fits in with national and sectoral strategies and with ongoing related activities in the project area;

-- describe present water supply and sanitation services in the project area and outline deficiencies in the services provided by both types of system;

-- relate present services to existing and future land use, taking account of any master plans which may exist for urban development;

-- confirm the existence of, or need for, a strategic plan to guide the long term development of water supply and sanitation services in the project area (list relevant background reports such as regional development plans, water resources studies and reconnaissance reports);

-- state the main objectives of the project and indicate the number and type of people to be served, the anticipated standards of service and expected conditions in the project area after the project is completed;

-- outline the proposed project components and possible alternative projects which could be implemented, in terms of both physical facilities and supporting activities (such as hygiene education, training and the like);

-- make a preliminary estimate of the local and foreign exchange costs of implementing and operating the preferred project. Indicate the most likely sources of capital and operating funds;

-- describe the institutional responsibilities for the pre-feasibility and feasibility study stages of project preparation, provide the cost estimates and suggest proposed sources of finance to carry out these studies;

-- indicate the likely institutional responsibilities for project implementation, operation and maintenance;

-- outline those policy issues which need to be resolved before the project can proceed;

-- set out the preliminary terms of reference for the pre-feasibility and feasibility stages of project preparation;

-- include a schedule for all future stages of project preparation, showing the earliest date when the project might be operational;

-- make recommendations for future action.

47.   The project identification report should be brief. Even so, it will be useful to summarize its contents. This can conveniently be done by following the format of the "Project Data Sheet" developed by the World Health Organization which is presented in Annex 2 together with instructions for its completion. The Project Data Sheet can be used to inform a large number of agencies having a possible interest in the project. The first Case Study in Volume 2 of these Guidelines provides a model of a project identification report incorporating the Project Data Sheet.

C. GUIDELINE FOR PRE-FEASIBILITY REPORT

Preamble

48.   The decision by an external agency to finance a project is usually based on the findings of a comprehensive feasibility study which shows that the proposed project is the "least cost" solution and is technically and institutionally feasible, financially viable, socio-culturally acceptable and economically justified.   But feasibility studies are expensive and require intensive effort and, therefore, should not be done until a preliminary screening and ranking of alternatives is made to show the relative merits of the project proposed for implementation.   The pre-feasibility study may be a separate and discrete stage of project preparation or it may simply be the first stage in a comprehensive feasiiblity study.

49.   The pre-feasibility report fulfills the screening function by selecting a preferred project for near-term implementation after considering:

-- longer-term needs;

-- deficiencies in the existing system;

-- alternative system developments, involving sequences of alternative projects.

50.   The chief aim of this screening process, which is iterative, is to select a near-term project which is consistent with probable future developments and not to prepare a rigid master plan aimed at the long-term development of water supply and sanitation sector services. The long term perspective is required only to confirm that near term developments are consistent with a longer term strategy for improving services.   The long-term strategy has to change over time and so must be re-examined whenever a major development is to be implemented.

51.   As a result of this screening process the planner should be able to produce an outline of future developments which seem most appropriate to provide sector services in the longer term.   If the pre-feasibility study cannot readily determine the best single project for development in the near term, then the conclusion may be that two or more projects need to be analyzed further.

NOTE: In this case, the selection of the preferred project should be left until the feasibility stage.

52.   The essence of the pre-feasibility stage is the screening and ranking of all project alternatives to select the preferred project before the detailed feasibility evaluation continues. This logic should be followed whether the pre-feasibility report is a separate activity, is an interim report towards a full feasibility study, or is included with the findings of the feasibility stage in a single report.

53.   Data shortages and imperfections are bound to arise during pre-feasibility planning. Yet, a minimum amount of basic information is required, including topographic, geologic, hydrologic and behavioural data which can often be rapidly obtained on the basis of field observations and sampling or survey techniques. Planners who need to make judgments and assessments using limited data must acknowledge the uncertainties introduced into the conclusions of the report. Future data gathering activities should also be planned and, after approval, commenced.

NOTE: At this stage of project preparation, qualitative assessments can be as important as quantitative ones. Once again, the need to have projects prepared by experienced professionals with multidisciplinary backgrounds needs to be emphasized.

54.   The pre-feasibility study may be used to present a sector program, in which case a comprehensive feasibility study might not be necessary. This is because a sector program can cover implementation of a large number of small projects (in small towns and rural communities) for which complex feasibility and engineering studies are not warranted at the time when the investment decision is made. The pre-feasibility report for a sector program should focus on the topics outlined in paras. 24-30, including:

   -- institutional and organizational aspects;

   -- regional and local social structure (community and household);

   -- sub-project selection criteria;

   -- design criteria;

   -- the method of implementing the various sub-projects;

   -- responsibilities and financing of future operations and maintenance.

NOTE: Sub-project descriptions and designs would normally be provided within the pre-feasibility report for only for a representative sample of the communities to be covered by the program, but the institutional, financial and other aspects affecting project implementation need to be developed in some detail.

55.   The presentation of the pre-feasibility report can be simplified by attaching relevant background documentation (such as background data, studies, plans and other reports) and referring briefly to their contents. The format and contents of a typical pre-feasibility report are outlined hereafter, followed by comments on what should be covered in each section of the report.

56.   Experienced study managers often produce a draft outline of the report at the beginning of the study period. This focuses the attention of all project planners on the intended logic and framework for their activities. Such a report outline can also be a useful management tool in terms of assigning tasks, budgets and deadlines to team members.

NOTE: All members of the planning team need to agree on basic data, methodology and provisional results at all stages of the study, as discussed in paras. 37-39. Periodic meetings and interim discussion papers can be used to encourage such teamwork.

57.   The report format which follows is generally applicable but needs to be adapted and used flexibly for any specific project. Three different types of pre-feasibility reports are presented in the Case Studies of Volume 2 and none replicates the format of this Guideline precisely.

NOTE: Project planners have to plan their own reports, aware of the perspectives of the intended audience, as well as plan the particular project.

C. GUIDELINE FOR PRE-FEASIBILITY REPORT

Table of Contents

Table of Contents (continued)

EXECUTIVE SUMMARY

58.   The essence of the pre-feasibility report is summarized for individuals without the time or need to read the entire report. This summary should make a quick impact on the mind of the reader about the basic strategy and approach in preparing the project and the contents and logic of the report. A well written summary (including one or two simple maps) is needed to describe the proposed project and its impacts in the context of the country's or region's long term development program.

NOTE: This key section of the report may be the only one read by decision makers so it must be clear and concise.

I. INTRODUCTION

59.   This chapter briefly explains the reasons for the report and how it was prepared.

Project Genesis

60.   -- Describe how the proposed project idea was developed.

-- Indicate which agencies, have responsibility for the promotion of the project.

-- List and explain briefly previous studies and reports on the project (particularly the project identification report) prepared by others.

-- Make reference to related long-term plans for the sector, regional development, land use, water resources development, rural development, primary health care, etc.

Organization and Management of Study

61.   -- Explain how the present study was carried out.

-- Indicate which agencies are responsible for the various elements of work (for example government departments, other agencies and consultants) and their role in preparing the study.

-- Present a timetable for the study and indicate the level of effort.

Scope and Status of This Report

62.   — Explain how this pre-feasibility report fits in the overall process of project preparation.

      — Identify data limitations.

      — List interim reports or notes submitted during the pre-feasibility study and summarize any guidance provided by the responsible project authority.

      — Explain whether the pre-feasibility report is intended to be used to obtain approval in principle for the proposed project. If so, the report needs to be more comprehensive and less tentative in its conclusions than in cases where a feasibility study is already underway or expected to be initiated shortly after the pre-feasibility report is completed.

II. THE WATER SUPPLY AND SANITATION SECTOR

63.   This chapter (although highly desirable) is not an absolutely essential part of a pre-feasibility study. The advantage of such an overview, however, is that it provides the planner and the audience with a valuable perspective for all other projects and programs, and, once prepared, can be used for other contemporary pre-feasibility reports, needing only periodic updating. It would be preferable to have a separate sector report to which reference could be made. Such a report should be updated periodically by the government, independent of project activities, and would serve as a sector planning tool. The chapter outlined below is comprehensive enough so it could be used in the preparation of a separate sector report.

64.   This chapter should show that the proposed project supports national and sectoral development plans. In most countries this sectorial overview would have a national focus, but in some countries (where individual states are large or where the national government does not have the basic responsibility for sector services) the overview should be presented in the context of the individual state or particular region. General information should be given on:

      — national organizations;

      — operational effectiveness;

      — goals of the water supply and sanitation sector;

-- any overview which has already been done by a planning or sector ministry or an international agency.[1]/ (This chapter should only summarize the information in such a report.)

65.   If the sector perspective does not significantly affect decisions concerning the proposed project, this chapter should be presented as an annex to the report. Such a format could improve the logic of the project analysis and still present readers with the opportunity to review useful background information.

Country Background

66.   -- Describe the physical setting, major topographic features, climate, etc. and make reference to one or more attached maps.

    -- Define population and historic growth rates (giving sources of data) and regional distribution (illustrated graphically if possible).

    -- Provide data on the urban and rural population, particularly the proportion of rural and urban people and their respective rates of growth.

    -- Provide and comment on alternative projections of population in the future.

    -- Describe the levels of government and explain how responsibilities for water supply, sanitation, health and other relevant sectors are allocated between different government agencies.

Economic and Health Indicators

67.   -- Summarize the main features and principal sectors of the national economy.

    -- Provide information on the national trend in per capita income and differences in per capita income among various segments of the population.

----

[1]/   Such as the World Health Organization sector reports for health, water and sanitation, or the World Bank and regional bank reports on economic development.

-- Indicate the number and concentration of urban and rural poverty groups on the basis of defined criteria.

-- Discuss regional variations income or standard of living.

-- Cite public health indicators such as life expectancy, morbidity and mortality data (by region and urban/rural center) on water- and sanitation-related diseases.

-- Describe general health services, curative and preventive.

Water Resources and Control

68. -- Provide an overview of available surface and groundwater resources.

-- Provide an overview of the meteorologic and hydrologic data available and comment on their reliability.

-- Describe precipitation patterns and regional variations.

-- Describe water use by sector and by source.

-- Indicate present and future trends and discuss any problems of water scarcity by regions.

-- Discuss the legal and administrative arrangements for controlling the use of water.

-- Describe the methods of authorizing surface and groundwater abstractions and measures for preserving water quality.

-- Make a general assessment of water pollution problems (this should include an assessment of the main causes of water pollution and regional variations).

-- Comment on the adequacy of existing procedures for controlling water quality and minimizing pollution.

Sector Organization and Developments

69. -- Name and describe all government and non-government institutions which have an impact on:

o water supply;
o sanitation (excreta and wastewater disposal).

-- Also explain briefly the responsibilities for:

    o public health and health education;
    o drainage;
    o solid wastes disposal.

-- Provide detailed information on the institutions directly concerned with water supply and sanitation services including their:

    o purpose and goals;
    o operational responsibilities;
    o managerial capability;
    o staffing levels;
    o locations.

-- Give a breakdown of the total population by categories and define the institutional responsibilities of those organizations which provide water supply and sanitation services to each category.

-- Describe the processes by which sector projects are planned, financed, built and operated.

-- Summarize the availability of local goods and services and indicate which components of projects need to be obtained internationally.

-- Explain the role of both users and suppliers of water and sanitation services in operating and maintaining facilities and what part they play in selecting technology, organization and financial policies.

-- Comment on the adequacy of operation and maintenance and provide information on unaccounted-for water and the physical state of facilities.

-- Give information on activities such as health promotion and hygiene education which could provide valuable inputs to a water supply and sanitation project.

-- Describe the philosophy, procedures and results of financing the capital and operating costs of water supply and sanitation services.

-- Discuss existing and proposed arrangements for surveillance of water quality.

Present Service Coverage and Standards

70. — Define the "service coverage", the number of people served, and "service standards", the types of services (such as standpipes, house connections, latrines and sewers) of the water supply and sanitation systems. (Note that different technologies can provide the same service standards.)

— Estimate the number of systems for each service standard, separately for water supply and for sanitation, by regions.

— Discuss the patterns of availability of water supply and adequate sanitation services by region and by season. Also discuss service reliabilities.

— Indicate whether service standards and coverage differ between the urban and rural population.

— Provide general information on service standards and coverage to low income groups.

— Define which population groups are excluded from public services and why.

— Comment on the use of safe water supply and adequate sanitation facilities (do people use the facilities available or do they prefer "traditional" practices).

Sector Goals

71. — Describe the country's past record in setting and fulfilling sector goals.

— Explain the planning process which established these goals.

— Summarize sector objectives and the development strategy to provide safe water supply and adequate sanitation services (of various service standards such as standpipes, piped systems, protected shallow wells, etc.) to specific target populations in specified periods of time.

— Describe the institutional responsibilities for meeting development goals in the water supply and sanitation sector and outline the implied workload (year by year) for each institution.

-- Describe the national goals of the government during the International Drinking Water Supply and Sanitation Decade (1981-1990). Also describe existing information for monitoring and evaluating Decade progress.

-- Discuss existing and future major projects in the sector.

Staffing Requirements and Training Needs

72. -- Forecast sector staff (by categories of skill) needed to meet sector goals in the years ahead.

-- Compare future staff requirements with present staffing levels.

-- Comment on any required increase in staff. Outline existing programs for sector-related education and training. Suggest appropriate recruitment and training procedures, including those for women.

-- Comment on staff turnover rates and possible procecures to retain skilled and experienced staff.

Financial Implications

73. -- List and describe briefly all projects undertaken within the past ten years (by region) and estimate the total expenditure for each project.

-- Estimate total capital and recurrent expenditures and sources of finance for water supply and sanitation programs in the public and private sectors over the past ten years. Compare these expenditures with total public expenditures. Also compare past expenditures in water supply and sanitaiton with those in other sectors.

-- Indicate the order of magnitude of community participation in past water supply and sanitation projects in terms of contributions of materials and labour as well as money.

-- Comment on any changes in relative and absolute amounts of funds allocated to investment in the sector.

-- Refer to and, if appropriate, attach the current long-term national development plan and make specific reference to anticipated investments in the water supply and sanitation sector.

-- Make projections of finances (capital and recurrent) needed to meet sector goals in the years ahead by amount and as a percentage of national expenditure in the public sector.

-- Compare future plans for water supply and sanitation with those for other sectors.

-- Indicate probable sources of financing for future capital requirements, such as:

  o funds generated by sector revenues;
  o government loans and grants;
  o anticipated financing from national or international lending agencies.

-- Also indicate anticipated sources for recurrent cost requirements, in the light of financial policies for the sector.

Involvement of International Agencies

74. -- Explain the role of international agencies which have been active in the sector within the past ten years.

  -- Summarize the involvement of each agency and list all specific projects together with their total cost and the amount of any external contributions.

III. THE PROJECT AREA AND THE NEED FOR A PROJECT

75. This important chapter explains why a project is needed and tells the reader about:

  -- the project area and its people;

  -- the present water supply and sanitation services in the project area;

  -- the prospects for future development;

  -- the need to improve existing services.

76. The project area should be accurately defined:

  -- For a project in a metropolitan area an indication of the administrative boundary of the urban area or the service area of the utility is usually sufficient, unless some of the present or future population to be served by the project live outside the present boundary;

-- Where the project is to serve geographically dispersed groups (say, for example, a series of rural villages), then the project area would consist of the regional area encompassing the dispersed groups or several related areas.

77.   Even if the project will only provide a single service, (for example, water supply but not sanitation), this section of the report should describe present arrangements for all sector services. It is particularly important to discuss the impact of the project on other services. For example, water supply projects often result in the need for major improvements in sanitation. In practice the existing and future standard for one service directly affects feasible standards for another.[1] Even for minimum service, such as handpumps or standpipes in rural areas, some provision should be made for excreta and wastewater disposal. Discussion of plans for reuse or disposal should be a part of every report. Hence, the sanitation implications should be addressed even when the main focus of the report is a water supply project.

78.   All of the information outlined in this chapter is seldom available without major efforts at data collection. Study managers need to determine the available data and decide what data are required to support conclusions at the pre-feasibility stage. Sometimes very qualitative judgements have to suffice. In other cases some new data need to be collected as part of the study. Fieldwork is limited to that needed to confirm and correct existing information or, if data is scarce, to reconnaissance surveys. Sometimes provisional assessments made at the pre-feasibility stage have to be confirmed or modified later at the feasibility stage, following the collection and analysis of new data.

Planning Horizon

79.   The planning period (or planning horizon) is defined at the outset and the rationale for this time frame explained. This is the

---

[1]   For example, piped water supplies and house connections may not be appropriate where population densities are high, soil permeabilities low and sewers not affordable because the wastewater which would result would actually aggravate public health problems. Sewers, on the other hand, are not feasible without an assured supply of piped water.

period within which alternative long-term potential demands[1]/ for water supply and sanitation services are estimated. Alternative sequences of project development are considered to select the preferred project for implementation in the near term.

80.   A relatively long-term perspective is used to prepare the strategic plan for system developments, generally twenty years or more ahead. This period could be reduced somewhat in areas where populations are small or where they are expanding very rapidly. Such perspectives should take into account the desires of "modernization" from the community's perspective, which can be considered in terms of upgrading service standards as resources are available.

81.   The design period (which is usually much shorter than the planning horizon) for various project components is a separate matter. Present value analysis of the cost of adding service capacity at different stages in the future leads to the definition of design periods. Thus a wastewater treatment plant may be designed for a period of 8 years, meaning that its capacity will meet demands in 8 years time, after which it will have to be expanded by an extension which could have a different design period. This topic should be handled in conjunction with the search for least cost solutions, as explained in paragraphs 137 to 139.

Project Area

82.   -- Describe (geographically) the project area and make reference to an accurate map or several maps if more than one region is involved.

-- Discuss any special features (such as climate, topography, culture and migration) which affect or could affect the project design, implementation or operation.

-- Show (on the map) boundaries of relevant political and administrative jurisdictions.

-- Indicate any ethnic, cultural or religious settlement patterns which may have a bearing on the project proposals.

1/ These demands will of course depend on various factors, including technical options, socio-cultural preferences, the availability of local and outside funds and the community's willingness and ability to pay for services of different standards.

Population Patterns

83.   -- Estimate the population in the project area.

    -- Indicate the source of data or the basis for this estimate.

    -- Review previous population data, historic growth rates and causes.

    -- Provide a range of estimates for future population growth within the project area for the planning period and indicate the most probable growth rates.

    -- Name the source of these estimates and how they compare with past population growth trends.

    -- Discuss any differences between population trends within the project area and those for the entire country.

    NOTE: When population estimates are plotted on semi-logarithmic paper, the slope of the graph indicates the compound growth rate and simplifies the analysis.

    -- Discuss those factors likely to affect population growth rates.

    -- Analyze the probable locations of the total population within the project area at future intervals in time, for example, five, ten and twenty years ahead.

    -- Review and discuss any patterns of seasonal migration within the area.

    -- Discuss the implications of this growth pattern on housing and local infrastructure.

Economic and Social Conditions

84.   -- Give a general description of present living conditions for people of different socio-economic and ethnic groups, with photos as appropriate.

    -- Provide data on the number and location of residents in the project area according to income levels or other indicators of socio-economic studies.

-- Define and provide specific data such as the location, density and land tenure arrangements of poverty groups and ethnic concentrations within the project area and show on project area map.

— Provide information on housing conditions and relative proportions of owners and tenants.

— Provide data by age and sex on education, literacy, unemployment and underemployment, etc.

— Provide data and make projections on housing standards, particularly the number of people per dwelling in various parts of the project area.

NOTE: Information on population density and housing standards is essential to making reasonable projections of future water needs.

-- Outline studies of existing social conditions and their conclusions.

-- Analyze the health situation within the project area, paying particular attention to diseases related to water and sanitary conditions.

-- Provide data on infant mortality and life expectancy and compare these to figures for other parts of the country.

-- Discuss the most prevalent water- and sanitation-related diseases (including morbidity and mortality) in the project area and suggest how to control these. Also review the possible need for hygiene education.

-- Discuss status of relevant health care programs in the area as well as other projects (housing, rural development, etc.) with extension services which might relate to improvements in environmental sanitation.

-- Comment on local organizations including women's clubs and informal groupings, which might become active participants in water supply and sanitation.

Regional Development Prospects

85. — Give a brief description of the local economy and explain how the resource base affects residents of the region.

-- Compare the local economic situation (including standards of living) with the national economic situation.

-- Comment on the prospects for economic development in the region.

-- Discuss whether there are any linkages between improved sector services and general development prospects.

Existing and Future Land Use Patterns

86. -- Provide information on the history of land use controls and their enforcement. Comment on their effectiveness and whether there are any changes expected in the near future.

-- Provide a map of the project area showing the existing categories of land use (industrial, agricultural and public lands should be clearly demarcated) and the major elements of infrastructure.

NOTE: The map should also show the locations of different residential areas (preferably by population density) to permit a ready understanding of population locations with locations of poverty and ethnic groups clearly indicated. Note any relevant settlement patterns by ethnicity or religion.

-- Provide information on master plans for future land use in the project area and comment on the likelihood of implementing these plans. Provide maps showing future probable land use developments.

-- Discuss how water supply and waste disposal services affect urban or regional development plans and their implementation. Where such plans do not exist or are inadequate, ensure that projected water and sanitation systems are consistent with sound urban development strategies.

Sector Institutions

87. -- Discuss the role and responsibility of all institutions (government and non-government) involved in water supply and sanitation services in the project area. Also discuss institutions providing related services such as urban upgrading, health, adult education, extension, etc.

-- Explain statutory boundaries or other limits which affect these institutions.

-- Describe which non-engineering organizations (such as public health agencies, regional planning agencies and community organizations) are involved in services connected with water supply and sanitation in the project area.

-- Briefly review the past performance of each institution involved in water supply and sanitation sector programs and assess the main constraints (political, financial, staff), if any, on their operations.

-- Comment on cooperation among sector institutions in planning, building, operating and using water supply and sanitation services.

-- Describe cooperation among the beneficiary population and informal organizations (such as women's clubs, cooperatives, credit associations and irrigation associations) which might be useful in project implementation.

Available Water Resources

88.   -- Summarize the quantity and quality of surface and groundwater resources, actual and potential, in the project area and vicinity. Comment on the quality and reliability of available data.

-- Outline existing studies concerning the development of potential sources including the reuse of wastewater.

-- Describe the existing patterns of water use by all sectors (industrial, domestic, agriculture, energy, etc). Identify supply surplus or deficiency and possible conflicts over the use of water, present or future.

-- Describe possible pollution problems which affect available surface and groundwater resources.

-- Summarize the role of various agencies in managing water resources, particularly water allocation and water quality control.

NOTE: Data and other background information should be presented in annexes.

Existing Water Supply Systems and Population Served

89.   This section should summarize and assess all existing water supply systems (both public and private) in the project area. Describe each system briefly with a narrative of its development.

-- Pay particular attention to the operating capacity of each system and component. Constraints on increasing services should be highlighted.

NOTES: i) Use maps, schematic diagrams, charts and tables of data to summarize information. Additional background material can be presented in an annex.

ii) If special attention has been paid to parts of the system (for example, an analysis of a treatment plant or distribution network by staff or by consultants), then the results should be summarized and reference should be made to more detailed reports.

90.   Explain and describe any non-potable water supply system in the project area, particularly systems developed for use by industries. Also discuss irrigation schemes which provide water for domestic purposes. Describe any impacts of such systems on the water resources used for potable water supplies, such as changes in groundwater levels or seasonal availability of surface sources.

91.   Describe the existing facilities for each water supply system, including:

-- water sources and the quantity and quality of each source, including local evaluation of quality, taste, and preferred use;

-- raw water headworks including conveyance systems such as raw water transmission mains;

-- water treatment facilities. Note any local attitudes concerning the use of chemicals in water treatment;

-- treated water reservoirs and pumping stations;

-- the transmission and distribution system (noting areas served and not served, with information on hours and standards of service, water pressures and operating problems);

-- flow metering arrangements for water produced by suppliers and water used by consumers;

-- the role of the private sector in delivering services (via boreholes, wells, pipelines, water vendors, etc.).

92.   Provide data, analysis and comments on the <u>service coverage</u> (numbers of people served) according to <u>service standards</u> (type of facility and quality of service) for each water supply system. Topics to be covered in this critical examination of the existing system are listed separately:

-- Estimate the number of people served by each water supply system:

  o unimproved systems:
    - shallow wells, rivers, lakes and, natural and man-made ponds,

  o improved point sources:
    - wells with pumps, rainwater storage tanks, etc.,

  o piped water systems (individual connections and standpipes);

-- For those people served by piped water systems, estimate the numbers of the following:

  o house connections (supplying indoor taps),

  o courtyard taps,

  o public standpipes;

-- For standpipes, provide general information to explain the convenience to consumers such as:

  o waiting times,

  o distance from homes,

  o availabilities within all ethnic areas,

  o existence of standpipes on both sides of roads,

  o types of containers used to carry water to homes,

  o use of standpipes by water vendors;

-- Estimate how many people are served by more than one source continuously or on a seasonal basis;

-- Note which sources are used for drinking, bathing, animals, etc;

— Describe those groups not being served by any improved water supply system (including those supplied by vendors, etc.) and explain why they do not receive any service;

— Describe how water is obtained, by whom, how much, etc. Children, women, men? Explain the preferred sources and use patterns of each group. Describe users' attitudes toward quality: preferences and constraints. Include anecdotal material which helps explain the use or non-use of certain sources;

-- Estimate the quantities of water used in each of the past five years by consumers in all groups, from all sources and for what purposes. Pay particular attention to the relatively large water users, including industries;

NOTE: Consumers should be categorized (to the extent that data permits) in terms of domestic, commercial, industrial and government users.

— Provide actual data or estimate, for each of the past five years, the following:

o the number of connections and estimated population served by each system,

o the number of connections with and without meters and the percentage of meters in working condition,

o the quantities of water produced from all sources,

o seasonal and daily peak factors,

o water sold to or used by all consumers,

o "unaccounted-for water" (that is, the difference between water produced and water known to be used by consumers),

o water tariffs;

-- Explain unaccounted-for water. Discuss trends and probable causes (physical losses, meter error, theft, inaccurate records, etc.) and efforts to reduce these losses;

-- Provide available water quality data (bacteriological and chemical analyses) for various sources of water supplied to the project area;

-- Include information on any system for rationing water (such as valve operations to limit supply during certain periods), on shortages and seasonal variations in supply;

-- Comment on the reliability of supply from various sources (by seasons) and estimate the amount of water that would be used (at present prices) if shortages did not exist;

-- Analyze the frequency of breakdowns, including the time taken to restore service;

-- Provide a special analysis of water supply and sanitation facilities serving the poorest people in the project area. Comment on how poor people use these facilities and how the present water supply arrangements affect the quality of life of poverty groups;

-- Provide a comprehensive critique of the various water supply systems, with particular comments on their weaknesses or problems and on possible means to overcome such problems. Refer to positive experiences with system facilities in the project area or nearby for guidance as to possible remedies to identified problems.

Existing Sanitation Systems and Population Served

93.   As in the case of water supply systems, this section should summarize and assess all existing sanitation and waste disposal systems in the project area and estimate the number of people each system serves. All methods used to dispose of human wastes and wastewater by all people in the project area should be described, including local sanitation systems and sewers.

-- Discuss with selected local informants (such as teachers or health workers) alternative technologies in light of socio-cultural, economic and technical constraints;

-- Pay particular attention to each method of waste disposal. Constraints on increasing services should be highlighted.

NOTE: Use maps, schematic diagrams, charts and tables of data to summarize information. Additional background material can be presented in an annex.

94.   Describe the <u>existing facilities</u> for each sanitation system, including:

-- the location of each system;

-- the history of the development of sanitation systems in the project area and the extent of all sewers carrying wastewater (with a distinction being made between separate sanitary and storm sewers and combined sewers);

-- information on legislation and regulations affecting the design, construction and operation of alternative types of sanitation facilities, such as regulations governing sewer and effluent quality, building codes and health regulations;

-- industrial wastewater discharges and disposal systems;

-- privately operated wastewater systems and treatment plants;

-- typical sketches of independent sanitation systems (latrines, septic tanks, etc);

-- estimates of the number of each type of sanitation systems and comments on their design, construction, operation and effectiveness;

-- informal reuse patterns of excreta if any (for pigs, fish, fertilizer, etc.);

-- the role of the private sector in providing services (such as septic tank emptying and nightsoil collection);

-- a description of existing wastewater treatment processes (including objectives, design criteria and operational effectiveness);

-- information on combined sewer overflows, treatment plant bypasses and frequency of use;

-- methods of disposing of effluents and sludges and information on the existing reuse of these waste products;

-- a comparison between the quantity of water used by all residents and industries and the amount of wastewater discharged through sewers;

-- an assessment of water quality in receiving bodies upstream and downstream of sewer outfalls.

95.   Provide data, analysis and comments on the <u>service coverage</u> (numbers of people served) according to <u>service standards</u> (type of facility and quality of service) for each <u>sanitation system</u>. This critical examination of the existing situation should cover the following topics:

— Provide a breakdown of the total population in the project area by groups according to the way in which they dispose of their body wastes:

  o primitive (defecation on the ground),

  o individual on-site sanitation facilities (latrines, septic tanks, etc.),

  o communal sanitation facilities,

  o sewerage;

-- Provide actual data or estimate, for each of the past five years:

  o the number of people using each sanitation system,

  o the number of sewer connections;

-- Review any social, cultural or religious considerations which may affect sanitation practices;

-- Describe any sanitation facilities which may have been provided and are not in use, explain why. Describe the actual disposal practices of such groups;

-- Discuss excreta disposal practices of children and note use of facilities in public buildings, especially schools;

-- Estimate the number of households which could be connected to the present sewer systems but are not, and explain the reasons;

-- Explain how sullage (greywater) from households not connected to sewers or septic tanks is disposed of;

-- Assess the effectiveness of the various sanitation systems in the project area in terms of:

o   costs,

o   effect on domestic hygiene and public health generally,

o   protection of water quality;

— Provide a special analysis of sanitation and waste disposal facilities serving the poorest people in the project area. How do people in poverty groups use these facilities? What impact do these arrangements have on their quality of life?

— Provide a comprehensive critique of the various sanitation systems and their use, with special emphasis on existing problems and on possible means to overcome such problems. Refer to positive experiences with sanitation facilities within the project area or in adjacent areas for guidance as to possible remedies to identified problems.

Drainage and Solid Wastes

96.   Briefly describe and analyze existing systems of stormwater drainage and solid waste (garbage) collection and disposal. This discussion should be focussed in terms of their impact on water supply and sanitation systems in particular and public health generally. Typical matters for consideration include:

-- quantities of wastewater, including sullage and seepage from septic tanks and latrines, in surface drains;

-- ultimate disposal of surface drainage and wastes therein;

-- drainage arrangements at public standpipes, laundry points, bathhouses and related water-use facilities;

-- interference caused by solid waste disposal practices in excreta and wastewater disposal systems and surface drains;

-- analysis of problems and alternative solutions;

-- institutional responsibilities for surface drainage and solid waste disposal, with reference to existing legislation and regulations;

-- existence of plans and programs to improve existing services, with outline of budgets and timetable and references to background reports or other documents.

Need for a Project

97.   This key section draws conclusions about the need for a project in light of population patterns and projections, existing service levels and standards, and prospects for improving and expanding existing systems. The first decision of the planner is whether a rehabilitation project is required immediately as well as major investments in new facilities. If the critical analysis of existing water supply and sanitation systems has indicated that major improvements in service can be obtained by remedying weaknesses in present systems, the first priority should be to make the necessary corrections. Planners should focus on this possibility from the outset and provide interim reports as required in order to initiate remedial action. National and international agencies are prepared to provide financial support if major investments or technical assistance are required to implement a rehabilitation project. In such cases a report on this topic should be produced as early in the planning process as costs and timetables for remedies can be reasonably estimated. If the recommended improvements are minor or not too expensive they can be implemented while progress continues on the pre-feasibility and feasibility studies.

NOTE: The Case Studies of Volume 2 provide two examples of how rehabilitation projects can be handled. In one example (Farmville), the pre-feasibility report recommends a project involving both immediate improvements and the construction of major new facilities. In another (Port City), a separate project of immediate improvements is recommended prior to completing the planning for a major new project.

98.   This final section of the chapter basically summarizes why the existing systems cannot cope with present and projected demands for services. The project which is to be recommended is to be defined in the next chapter, following an overview of the long term strategy for providing sector services in the project area. Topics to be considered here include:

-- a description of the consequences these deficiencies in water and sanitation services will have on the present and future population in the project area if major improvements are not made;

-- an outline of priorities to:

   o improve and expand water supply and sanitation services,

   o meet basic human needs as well as demands by industry and commerce;

-- an assessment of the need for hygiene education and the promotion of the use of water and sanitation services to improve public health in the project area;

-- comments on the urgency of project preparation and implementation.

IV. STRATEGIC PLAN FOR WATER SUPPLY AND SANITATION

99.   In this chapter alternatives for improving sector services throughout the planning period are proposed and evaluated. The main aim is to recommend a feasible and affordable project in the context of a phased development program for improving sector services. Planning for water supply and sanitation services ought to be carried out together because design criteria and technical alternatives for one inevitably affect the other.

NOTE: Where joint planning becomes complicated by differing institutional responsibilities, pragmatic arrangements should be made for pre-investment planning of water supply and sanitation services.

100.   For urban projects, the strategic plan for water supply and sanitation services should be consistent with reasonable plans for future urban development. If acceptable urban development plans do not exist, water supply and sanitation planners need to ensure that the strategic plan for this infrastructure encourages sound urban development.

101.   Existing basic information (for example, census records, topography, geology and water quantities) is used, although there are cases where certain additional data have to be specially obtained. Refined data are not required for pre-feasibility planning since quantified conclusions are expected to have a reasonable degree of uncertainty. Some socio-economic data may have to be estimated based on information collected from sample surveys. Since data requirements are modest, only limited fieldwork is usually necessary. However this report should highlight data deficiencies which need to be corrected when the comprehensive feasibility study is prepared.

102.   The strategic plan is prepared through an iterative process, by considering alternative development sequences to provide target service coverage and standards at affordable costs, both in economic and financial terms. The horizon for this long term planning of the system is generally twenty years ahead. The most important conclusion to emerge from the screening and ranking of alternative projects is the definition of the priority project to be implemented in the near term. This recommendation defines the "project" which is then planned in more detail during the feasibility stage (Section D).

103.   If a sector program is to be implemented, this chapter should describe:

-- how communities are selected;

-- in what order they will receive project benefits (selection criteria);

-- standard designs to be used;

-- cost recovery and affordability criteria;

-- institutional arrangements describing local responsibility and external support.

Objectives

104.   The main purpose of a strategic plan for water supply and sanitation services project is to provide for improved living conditions for people living in the project area. Related objectives are to support growth of industries, commercial enterprises and institutions such as schools and hospitals.

105.   Estimates should be provided of future service coverage, that is the number of people who will receive improved water supply and sanitation services, along with target dates showing when these various service coverage will be achieved.

106.   More general objectives should also be described and quantified, including those of:

-- regional development;

-- public health improvements;

-- institutional strengthening.

Water Supply Service Standards

107.   Needs-oriented planning for water supply projects is mainly concerned with the efficient delivery of water to "points of use" serving defined consumers and works backwards through the system to the water source. Specific consideration should be given to individual and independent water systems, such as wells or rainwater catchments and reservoirs, in addition to the water supply from the distribution network. Service standards for a network system include:

-- public standpipes;

-- yard taps;

-- house connections for internal plumbing.

These alternative service standards each result in different water use patterns which are assessed and aggregated to produce alternative total demands for water.

108.   Determining the most appropriate service standards, such as providing water through standpipes or house connections, is necessarily an interactive process since the choice depends on:

-- technical feasibility of alternatives;

-- public health implications of alternatives;

-- implications for sanitation;

-- minimization of capital and operating costs of water supply and sanitation services;

-- total capital requirements and possible constraints;

-- charges for services and affordability for the consumer;

-- social feasibility, especially consumer preferences.

NOTE: Water supply service standards can be upgraded over time. An area initially served by standpipes, for example, can be served by yard or house connections by expanding the capacity of the distribution system.

109.   This section discusses the various options which have been considered (including, in some instances, no improvements over existing conditions) and reports on the preliminary analysis which results in selected service standards (certain areas may be supplied solely by standpipes, others by individual taps, etc.) for different areas or districts within the community. Source development and transmission facilities are planned accordingly.

Sanitation Service Standards

110.   Needs-oriented planning for sanitation projects is mainly concerned with the living conditions of the people in the project area, particularly the way in which they dispose of body wastes and wastewater. To understand needs and preferences, it is important to discuss options with knowledgeable local residents.

111.   A wide range of sanitation technologies is available, as illustrated on Figure 2. The technical feasibility of alternative sanitation systems depends heavily on water supply services in the area, on population densities, on soil permeability and hydrogeological conditions.

112.   Upgrading of sanitation systems is possible over time and should be considered in system planning. Figure 3 illustrates how alternative sanitation technologies can be upgraded. It also shows the various service standards of water supply which can be accommodated by alternative sanitation technologies.

113.   As in the case of water supply projects, the way in which the most appropriate sanitation service standards are determined is the result of interactive assessments involving:

-- technical feasibility of alternatives;

-- public health implications of alternatives;

-- implications for water supply;

-- minimization of capital and operating costs of water supply and sanitation services;

-- total capital requirements and possible constraints;

-- charges for services and affordability for the consumers;

-- social feasibility, especially consumer preferences.

114.   This section of the report should discuss the various service standards and technical options which have been considered and which form the basic criteria for planning the total sanitation system.

Community Preferences and Affordability

115.   Water and sanitation systems which are not wanted by the people for whom they are intended will not be properly used or maintained and will not produce the desired benefits. Therefore, representatives of the   intended beneficiaries should be consulted during project planning. However, the planners consulting with the beneficiaries need to make clear the technical choices and the fact that the costs and associated charges for services increase with higher service standards. Consumer preferences must be understood so that the planners can recommend realistic service standards after considering various options. Women as well as men should be involved in these exchanges of information.

GENERIC CLASSIFICATION OF SANITATION SYSTEMS BASED ON DISPOSAL METHODS

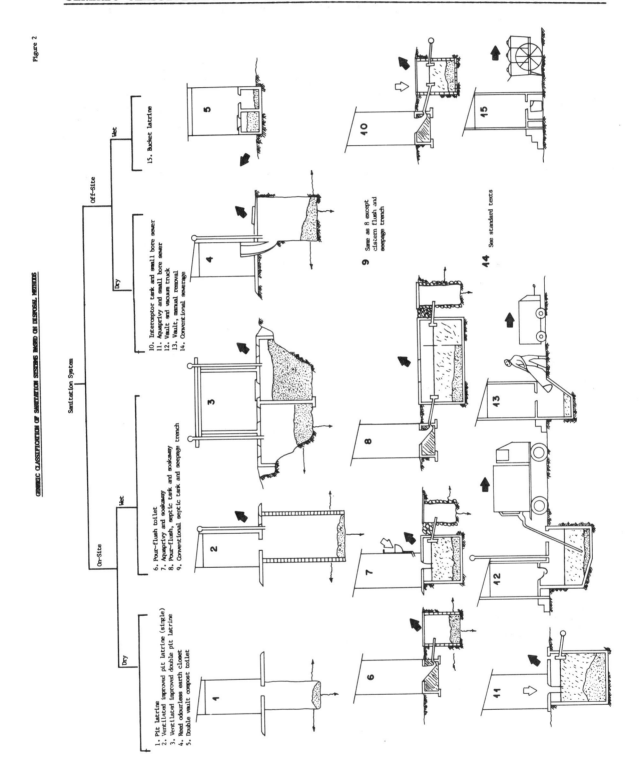

POTENTIAL SANITATION SEQUENCES

Figure 3

Sanitation technology	Water Service Standard		
	Hand carried	Yard tap	House connection
Double vault compost toilet			
Vault and vacuum truck	(Unlikely)		
Ventilated improved pit latrine or Reed odourless earth closet			(Unlikely)
Pour-flush toilet or aquaprivy			
Small bore sewer with interceptor tanks			
Conventional sewer or septic tank	(Not Feasible)	(Unlikely)	

NOTE: Consulting the potential users of the systems can lead to expectations of improvements which can seldom be provided immediately. Special guidance needs to be given to interviewers to avoid creating future problems with project beneficiaries.

116. Projects must be selected which are affordable to the people they serve. Local beneficiaries should meet recurring costs for at least operation and maintenance, and usually (depending on local income levels and government policies) pay somewhat higher charges for use above minimum service in order to repay capital costs or to make funds available for further system improvements.

117. This section of the report must discuss the ability and willingness of people in the project area to pay for improved sector services. Examine:

-- existing tariff policies and practices;

-- user costs for alternative systems;

-- incomes of various groups of people in the project area;

-- the ratio of water and sanitation charges to the total income of various groups in the project area.

118. Information should also be provided on what role the local community played in considering alternative water supply and sanitation systems and what their preferences are for one or more alternatives and what contributions they can make in time, effort or cash.

Capital Availability

119. Planners should remember that availability of funds is one of the prime factors that will ultimately determine the scope and scale of a feasible project. Therefore, at the outset, some effort should be made to ascertain from the appropriate agency the order of magnitude of funding likely to be made available and the probable sources. Other perspectives on this matter are discussed in terms of the financial feasibility of the project (paras. 150-154).

Future Demands for Water Services

120. Describe and quantify the projected needs for water supply throughout the planning period. The purpose is to determine the amount of water which is required to meet alternative service standards and service coverage over the years ahead. These demands then form the basis for planning the technical solutions to providing system requirements.

121.   Of course an iterative process is required in order to present reasonable projections of future water demands. Each iteration considers specifically the numbers of consumers to be provided with each standard of service in the years ahead. Alternative standards need to be considered (paras. 107-109). Water supply standards should be linked directly to sanitation standards and considered together in this planning.

122.   In each year the total needs for water have to be estimated, taking into account probable tariffs. First to be estimated are the demands which can be supplied by point source (e.g. wells or rainwater catchments) at lower cost than through piped systems. Then the water to be provided by the distribution network is estimated by categories of consumer, usually:

> -- domestic, including:
>
> > o standpipes,
> > o yard connections,
> > o house connections;
>
> -- industrial and commercial;
>
> -- government;
>
> -- other significant categories.

123.   The number of water connections is a critical factor affecting the quantity of water used. Thus estimates of future water needs should include estimates of the numbers of connections of different types. Correlations between future water use and numbers of connections should be compared to present and previous years and rationalized.

Future Demands for Sanitation Services

124.   Define and determine the projected requirements for various types of sanitation facilities in each future year with due consideration for all reasonable alternative standards (paras. 110-114). Factors to be considered include:

> -- population locations and densities;
>
> -- water supply per capita and per unit of area;
>
> -- local soil conditions and slopes.

125.   Determining the numbers of people to be served each year by different sanitation service standards and technologies is an iterative process in which population patterns, water use habits, costs of

alternative systems, consumer preferences, and affordability must all be considered. The result of this analysis is a summary, year by year, of the numbers of people to be serviced by each sanitation system. Another result is an estimate of the numbers of facilities of each type which need to be built each year.

126.   Consistency and coordination has to be maintained between projections for both water supply and sanitation services. Data have to be generated by local areas to ensure that the basic assumptions (number of people, housing units, population densities, numbers of connections, etc.) are consistent and rational for both services.

Strategic Plan for Water Supply and Sanitation

127.   This section determines the preferred development sequence for the water supply and sanitation system. It examines and compares alternative development sequences to overcome existing deficiencies and meet peoples' present and future needs for these services. Each sequence will typically consist of a series of system improvements and expansions to be implemented over the planning horizon, of say, the next twenty years. The recommended project will then consist of those components of the optimum water supply and sanitation development sequence which can be implemented in the near term.

128.   The screening process ensures that the project recommended for development in the near future forms part of the least cost solution for the long term development of the system. The screening process therefore involves:

   -- identifying alternative development sequences for the water supply and sanitation systems;

   -- comparing the present value of the capital and operating costs of each sequence in order to determine the least cost solution as discussed in paras. 137-139.

NOTE: Normally strategic plans are prepared separately for the water supply and sanitation systems, though the two are obviously interlinked and cannot be developed in isolation.

129.   A key task in preparing the strategic plan is to determine priorities because not all needs can be satisfied in the immediate future. Those target groups to be served first must be defined and, in so doing, those who have to wait longer for service improvements are also defined. Special attention should be paid to the needs of low income groups and to the resource tradeoffs associated with providing services to them. The criteria for forming the basis for these recommendations have to be made explicit.

130.   Consider alternative types of improvement when recommending priorities and stages for development. Pay particular attention to opportunities to rehabilitate existing facilities because such work can usually be done relatively quickly and inexpensively. Of course the reasons that the facilities are not operating satisfactorily need to be determined so the basic problems, usually institutional, can also be remedied.

131.   Analyzing the capacity of the major elements of the water supply and sanitation systems helps to determine the constraints in the existing facilities. Alternative methods of overcoming the constraints are then examined in order to find the least cost solution and identify components which need to be improved immediately. This evaluation of constraints is sometimes referred to as "bottleneck analysis."

132.   Preparing the strategic plan for water supply begins with target service coverage and defined service standards. For piped water systems the planning next concentrates on water sources, after due consideration of:

-- projected water needs, by years, for the entire system (paras. 120-123);

-- realistic allowances for unaccounted-for water between water sources and consumers;

-- peaking factors (daily and seasonal).

133.   Water system planning involves considering the capacity and development cost of:

-- reductions in water losses which can be justified economically, by deferring the development of new sources;

-- alternative water sources, surface and groundwater, with particular emphasis on maximizing the use of all existing water sources;

-- alternative treatment transmission systems (pipelines and pumping stations) from the sources to the distribution systems;

-- distribution systems, including pipe networks, reservoirs and pumping stations, to reach all consumers;

-- providing alternative service standards in future, including the upgrading of existing facilities, and planning the system for such expansion.

134.   Preparing the strategic plan for <u>sanitation</u> is generally more difficult than for water supply because of the wider range of technical choices (service standards) and the probability of consumer preferences changing over time. On-site sanitation systems are technically simple and their possible use should be considered before off-site systems.

135.   Determining the capacities and development costs of off-site systems begins with the definition of the quantities and locations of wastes to be removed. The system components whose capacity and costs have to be estimated include those for:

    -- treatment and disposal (treatment plants);

    -- collection systems (sewers or other forms of transport).

NOTE: Any analysis of existing or proposed sewer systems requires a thorough analysis of stormwater drainage in the project area.

136.   Strategic planning involves the definition of all inputs needed to achieve the target service levels. This involves preparing preliminary designs of all physical facilities for water and sanitation. No less important is the design of the supporting activities: hygiene education, staff training, institutional improvements, etc.

137.   Once alternative development sequences for water supply and sanitation systems have been identified, they are evaluated to determine the <u>least cost solution</u>. This involves:

    -- expressing all costs (capital and operating) for each year in economic terms;

    -- discounting future costs to present values;

    -- selecting the sequence with the lowest present value.

Costs are expressed in economic terms because the decision among alternatives should reflect their resource cost to the economy as a whole, not their financial cost to whichever people or agencies pay for them. Therefore costs should be in constant prices (free of inflation), with transfer payments such as taxes eliminated and shadow prices employed for resources whose market prices are distorted and do not reflect their relative scarcity in the economy (typically unskilled labor, capital, energy, and foreign exchange). Sometimes, there are major discrepancies between the financial and economic cost ranking of sequences. In such cases, the project proponents should attempt to obtain a specific subsidy from the government to permit the selection of the optimal economic alternative. If this is impossible, consideration will have to be given to selecting a less than optimal economic alternative simply because it may prove less costly in financial terms. This will, however, represent a net waste of resources for the economy as a whole.

138.   Discounting all future costs to the present is done to reflect the different cost to the economy of resources used at different future dates. An expenditure of $ x ten years from now has a present value of less than $ x today. Correspondingly, an expenditure of $ x in fifteen years time will have an even lower present value. The discount rate used in calculating the present values of economic costs for comparing alternative development sequences is the opportunity cost of capital, which is a shadow price reflecting the scarcity of capital in the economy.

139.   This process of screening alternative systems development sequences is referred to as least cost or cost-effectiveness analysis. It results in the ranking of alternative sequences, the elimination of unrealistic and infeasible projects, and the selection of an optimum development sequence consisting of the staged development of a series of feasible projects.

140.   Definition of the strategic plan for water supply and sanitation over the planning period concludes this section. The plan definition should include maps to show the staged development of the systems and estimates of capital costs for each service over the years ahead.

V. PROPOSED WATER SUPPLY AND SANITATION PROJECT

Project Definition

141.   The project comprises those components of the strategic plan for the water supply and sanitation systems which can be implemented in the near term (the next three to four years). The project would consist of:

-- the rehabilitation of existing water supply and sanitation facilities and institutional procedures;

-- construction of water supply and sanitation facilities to improve and expand the existing systems;

-- a package of support activities such as public motivation, education and training required to plan, construct, operate and maintain the systems;

-- equipment and other measures for the effective operation and maintenance of the existing and expanded systems;

-- any consulting services needed for:

    o completion of the feasibility study,
    o project implementation,
    o planning the next project in the development sequence;
    o meeting specific objectives such as accounting improvements, staff training, water loss reduction, etc.,
    o support activities.

142.   Thorough documentation should be provided to describe all components of the project, including:

-- location maps and engineering drawings;

-- preliminary technical information for each major component;

-- an implementation schedule with realistic allowances for all steps up to the initial operation of each component;

-- costs expressed on a year-by-year basis for building and operating each component of the project. These cost estimates should be presented in both constant prices and in current prices to allow for expected inflation.

NOTE: While the selection of an optimum development sequence involved economic costs, the recommended project will have to be financed at market prices. Its cost estimate is therefore presented in expected current prices, with allowances for inflation.

143.   At this pre-feasibility stage, there is no need to examine the project's environmental and social aspects in detail. It is, however, necessary to ensure that no major problems will be encountered which would jeopardize the feasibility of the project. Thus major environmental aspects like water withdrawals and wastewater disposal must be considered. Also major social aspects like the acceptability of new technologies and the displacement of people.

Institutional Responsibilities

144.   No project is feasible unless it can be planned, built and finally operated to provide the intended services. It is essential that procedures adopted to meet this goal do not drain resources, especially staff, away from the continued operation and maintenance of existing facilities. This section of the report takes an initial look at the means by which responsibilities for the various activities will be determined and implemented.

145.   The institutional arrangements are important for any single project. The pre-feasibility report must pay particular attention to this topic for sector programs, which involve several individual projects, because of the emphasis on various organizations which will carry out such a program (paras. 27 and 54).

146.   If the pre-feasibility study is intended to conclude with a report on the basis of which the investment decision for the project will be made, explain how project feasibility will be confirmed and who will be responsible for completing all necessary planning.

147.   Explain the proposed arrangements to complete the design and construction of the project. This involves several points:

-- Identify all agencies and groups (government and non-government) which need to be involved in project implementation. Specifically consider whether construction will be carried out by the private sector or the public sector;

-- Name the lead agency which will coordinate all necessary inputs and identify mechanisms which will be used to ensure effective leadership;

-- Diagnose existing weaknesses in institutions to be involved, explain how they are likely to affect project implementation and propose suitable remedies;

-- Note participation of women in different institutions, especially in jobs as extension agents, community workers, etc;

-- Specify the role of each agency or group and estimate the human and financial resources each will require in order to ensure efficient project implementation;

-- Examine requirements for skilled and unskilled labor to construct the project and compare these to the human resources available in the project area;

-- Pay particular attention to opportunities to develop local support for the project, including providing information about such benefits as improved health, convenience, and privacy for sanitation;

-- Review the ways in which people in the project area could contribute in cash or in kind towards project planning and construction.

148.   Even if the project is well planned and built, services will not be provided unless careful attention is paid from the outset to project operation and maintenance. Frequently, the agency or group involved in the operational stage of the project is different from the agency or group which manages project design and construction, particularly in rural schemes.

149.   For this part of the report the planner must:

— Determine all resources needed to operate the project, including managerial and logistical services involving communications, spare parts, chemical and energy supplies, specialist skills, etc. Examine alternative sources for these resources in the public and private sectors;

— Consider the potential role of project area residents in operation and in maintenance;

— Assess staff requirements in all relevant groups and at all skill levels and compare these to the supply of human resources available to operate and maintain the project;

— Devise suitable recruitment, training and incentive programs so that qualified staff will be ready to operate the facilities once construction is completed;

— Ensure that the ultimate users, often women, know how to effectively use and operate the improved facilities, including how to maintain, repair or obtain help.

NOTE: Recruitment and training of male and female staff for the operational stage, including personnel for working with communities, should be carried out well before the completion of project construction.

Financial Aspects

150.   Comprehensive financial analyses are expected at the feasibility stage for major projects, particularly those of agencies dependent on revenues generated by providing project services. Nevertheless attention must also be paid at the pre-feasibility stage to critical financial questions. First, the financial viability of the project entity is examined. Then, the basic questions concerning the project are answered, including how funds can be provided for the capital costs of the project and how recurrent expenditures can be met once the project is operational.

151.   Define the capital costs to complete the design and construction of all project components, including support activities. Costs should be estimated on an annual basis throughout the implementation period, with due regard for the construction schedule and allowances for physical contingencies. Estimate the foreign exchange component of the capital costs. Explain the price level in which basic cost estimates are prepared (usually the current year or the year before the report is prepared). Then estimate the anticipated price increases in each year during the construction period so that future costs can be escalated accordingly. The final cost estimate is the total cost for which the project can actually be built and determines how much money must be secured at the outset of the implementation period.

152.   Prepare a provisional financing plan for the project to illustrate all sources of funds to pay for the estimated capital costs. Possible sources to be considered include:

-- cash generated by the project authority from the sale of services during the project period (before the new systems are operational);

-- capital contributions from voluntary organizations and foundations or from consumers of future services;

-- loans from national credit institutions such as banks, pension and life insurance funds;

-- loans or grants from regional or national governments;

- loans or grants from international sources such as banks, bilateral agencies and multilateral agencies.

153.   The question of interest during construction should be considered in conjunction with the financing plan. If lending agencies agree, the interest payments on loans can be deferred until the project facilities become operational and capable of generating revenue. In such cases the interest would be capitalized and the initial loan amount would be increased accordingly.

154.   Examine the proposed project, its capital cost and the financing plan to determine whether or not the resource requirements are reasonable from two different perspectives. Will the project claim an unreasonably large share, in per capita terms or in aggregate, of the national resources available for the water supply and sanitation sector throughout the country? In the region where the project will be built, will the proposed investment claim an unreasonable share of infrastructure or public sector investments? The project may not be feasible and may have to be reconsidered if the answer to either of these basic questions is positive.

155.   Prepare estimates of all recurrent costs during the first few years of operation of the project. These costs should cover all expenditures of the principal operating agency for the entire system, including the project, to determine the future financial health of the agency. The future financial situation of several agencies has to be examined if more than one is to be responsible for delivering sector services. Expenditure categories should cover:

-- staff wages and benefits;

-- chemicals and energy required to operate the system;

-- spare parts and other materials for system maintenance;

-- transportation and administrative expenses;

-- other costs associated with operating and maintaining the system.

156.   The principal sources of operational revenue are the present and future tariffs for the sale of water supply and sanitation services. Provide information on the financial objectives of tariff policies, including a discussion of methods for determining tariffs and the process by which tariffs are changed. Indicate past and present tariffs. Suggest appropriate future tariff policies and resulting tariff levels.

157.   Lending agencies, whether national or international, need to be persuaded that any loans made for the project can be repaid. Accordingly the pre-feasibility report should indicate that the project authority's future revenues can meet all expenditures, including loan repayments. The degree of information required to demonstrate this point should be discussed in advance with potential lenders since it depends on their policies as well as on the normal accounting policies and practices of the agency which will operate the project. Simplified projections of future income statements might suffice, provided more detailed financial projections (including balance sheets and cash flows) are to be provided at the feasibility stage.

VI. CONCLUSIONS AND RECOMMENDATIONS

158.   This chapter informs decision makers of the essential results of the pre-feasibility report, including the next steps necessary to develop a project.

Conclusions

159.   Provide a brief summary of the results of the pre-feasibility study, including:

-- review of the need for the project, alternatives considered, and recommended strategic plan for long term development of water supply and sanitation systems;

-- designation of project concepts explored, found unattractive and thus recommended for dropping from further consideration;

-- explanation of priorities concerning target groups and areas to be served within the project period;

-- definition of recommended project for implementation, including capital costs and implementation schedule;

-- tentative financing plan for project costs and implications for future tariffs;

-- summary of potential benefits of proposed project and of supporting programs;

-- comments on possible urgency associated with the proposed initial project;

-- recommendations for dealing with lower priority needs that will not be met during the project period.

160.   Conclusions made at the pre-feasibility stage are, necessarily, based on a preliminary analysis of data which are incomplete and not totally reliable. Planners should make decision makers aware of this by emphasizing the data limitations and other factors which make the conclusions provisional. All areas of uncertainty should be highlighted. Explanations should be provided of plans to obtain better data and confirm and modify these tentative conclusions during the feasibility stage.

Issues and Risks

161.   A major objective of the pre-feasibility stage of project investment is to identify and resolve potential problems that could endanger the success of the project. Possible issues and risks should be identified, such as:

-- boundary questions for project area or involved agencies;

-- water availability and the possible need for sharing resources with adjacent regions and other users;

-- the availability of land for project facilities;

-- difficulty in planning and implementating water supply and sanitation services at the same time because of different institutional responsibilities. Also potential problems in having project area residents utilize improvements in both these basic services;

-- problems in coordinating engineering inputs and supporting activities in project development;

-- the unwillingness of local leaders to consider alternative standards of service or legal/administrative difficulties associated with alternative technologies;

-- land tenure questions which could affect project area residents' willingness to upgrade their properties;

-- the attitudes of the ultimate users toward alternative service standards;

-- the possible need to change policies for charging for sector services based on the ability and willingness of beneficiaries to pay for them;

-- shortage of labor or materials for project construction or of trained local personnel for community motivation or hygiene education;

-- uncertainty of the supply or price of basic project inputs (for example, energy);

-- alternative sources of finance (national and international) and implications in terms of timing and administrative procedures;

-- prospects for future maintenance of the improved facilities, both the community system and the household components.

Recommended Actions

162.   All actions necessary to complete project preparation and implementation should be identified. In doing so:

-- Name the party responsible for each recommended action;

-- Estimate the probable cost;

-- Present a suggested timetable for action.

At the same time as the proposed project is prepared, project authorities should be encouraged to take immediate action to rehabilitate existing water supply and sanitation facilities and the systems by which they are operated and maintained. This immediate action program should be identified and costed separately from recommendations for further preparation of the proposed project.

163.   Typical activities which would be recommended at this stage could include:

i) Identification of data collection programs which need to be completed for the feasibility stage and recommend actions as to how and when the necessary data should be obtained.

ii) Demonstrations of the feasibility of technologies or service standards which may be new to the project area.

164.   Provide a realistic schedule for all future stages of project preparation and implementation. In preparing such a schedule due consideration must be given to all groups whose inputs and decisions can affect the project and its timing. Such groups can include:

-- the agency or agencies responsible for the pre-feasibility and feasibility studies;

-- national authorities responsible for financial matters, including perhaps the planning and budget organizations;

-- local, regional or national authorities who must endorse or approve the project at various stages;

-- sources of capital finance, including international as well as national organizations.

NOTE: Project feasibility can be determined on the basis of preliminary designs but more detailed designs are usually necessary for procurement and construction. In order to avoid subsequent delays in project implementation, attention should be drawn in the pre-feasibility report to detail designs which should commence in the feasibility stage so that construction of priority components can commence as soon as the feasibility study has been approved.

D. GUIDELINE FOR FEASIBILITY REPORT

Preamble

165.   Financing agencies, both internal and external, generally decide whether to support a proposed project based on the information provided in a comprehensive feasibility report. For this reason, a feasibility study requires more intensive analysis and more reliable information than that presented in the pre-feasibility study.

166.   As indicated earlier, pre-feasibility and feasibility studies can be combined into one report. These Guidelines recognize this possibility but separately cover the analyses required for each.

167.   The basic aim of the pre-feasibility report is to select a project which can improve water supply and sanitation services at minimum cost in the near term, while fitting logically into the strategic plan for the longer term development of these systems. At the feasibility stage the focus is concentrated on the near term project.

168.   Sufficient data collection and analysis are required to confirm that the project is feasible in all senses. It has to be demonstrated to be socially, economically, technically, financially, environmentally and institutionally feasible. Experience and judgement are required to determine how much data need to be collected for the feasibility report, since data collection and analysis are expensive and time-consuming. The general rule is that new data are only collected when they can influence the decisions to be taken during the feasibility study. Detailed information required to construct the project facilities can be obtained during the implementation stage.

169.   Although the feasibility study generally concentrates on a specific project option selected on the basis of a previous pre-feasibility study, there may be cases where two separate but competing project options appear (at the pre-feasibility stage) to be equally attractive for implementation. In such cases, both projects should be assessed up to the point where one project is evaluated to be superior, at which time preparation of the superior project (or chosen alternative) continues and work on the inferior one is stopped. Occasionally the proposed project (the superior one) proves not feasible when reviewed in detail. In such an event, this information should be announced as soon as it is confirmed so that an alternative project can be prepared with minimal loss of time and resources.

170.   Project appraisal and the investment decision are based on the feasibility report. This means that the feasibility study must advance all planning (including, if possible, detailed engineering for priority components of the project) to the point that implementation can begin as soon as funding is provided.

171.   Different financing agencies have different requirements concerning the degree to which designs need to be completed before the project can be approved. They may also have other specific requirements on topics such as procurement. To avoid misunderstanding and loss of time, the project planners should discuss their particular requirements with the potential financing agencies at the outset of the feasibility study.

172.   The project feasibility report should be presented clearly in one or two volumes with additional information and data provided in supplementary documentation as appendices to the main volume. It is particularly important to record all new data collected during (and at the expense of) the feasibility study, as well as its analysis. However, the report itself should concentrate on the results of the analysis and not on data collection and methods of analysis.

173.   The following report format is generally applicable but needs to be adapted for each specific project. The Case Study of Volume 3 provides an example of a comprehensive feasibility study for a specific water supply and sanitation project in an urban environment. However, neither the format of that example nor of this Guideline should be replicated for any particular project. Instead the project planner must analyze the purpose and audience for the report for the project in question and design the study and the presentation of its results accordingly.

D. **GUIDELINE FOR FEASIBILITY REPORT**

EXECUTIVE SUMMARY

174.   The most important results of the feasibility study should be summarized for the convenience of individuals, particularly decision makers, who may not read the entire report. The summary should be written concisely and should include one or two simple location maps to present the proposed project clearly.

175.   The summary should tell:

-- why the study was conducted;

-- what aspects were considered;

-- what was determined;

-- what action should be taken.

I. BACKGROUND

176.   This chapter should describe the history of the proposed project and explain how it fits into the national sector strategy and the long term development program for water supply and sanitation services.

177.   The contents of this chapter depend largely on the context of this report within the process of project preparation, specifically the relationship of this report to the pre-feasibility report. Questions which must be answered in this chapter include:

-- Does a separate, pre-feasibility report exist? When was it prepared? Is it accepted as reliable? Does it provide information not included in the feasibility report (in which case it must be preserved and read in conjunction with the present report)?

-- Have the pre-feasibility and feasibility reports been prepared without interruption by the same group of planners?

-- Are the assumptions and basic data in the pre-feasibility report entirely consistent with those in the feasibility report? If not, changes should be highlighted.

-- What instructions have project planners received since the original terms of reference? How have such

instructions affected the process of project preparation
and the results of the feasibility study?

178.   When the feasibility report is completed independently from
the pre-feasibility report, or after an interval of a year or more, the
history of previous studies (including the pre-feasibility study) should
be summarized. Also the study organization and management. Refer to
the first chapter of the pre-feasibility report (paras. 59-62) for
guidance.

179.   Other reports which must be read in conjunction with this one
should be listed. If, on the other hand, all substantive conclusions
from previous reports are accepted and incorporated within the present
feasibility report, references to previous work need only be made in the
appropriate section of this report.

II. THE PROJECT AREA AND NEED FOR A PROJECT

180.   This chapter of the feasibility report is only necessary to
present information and analyses which were not included in the
pre-feasibility report. In this case the format and logic of the
earlier report (paras. 76-98) can be used. It is important to highlight
any changes which result from the new information. Descriptive material
can be placed in an annex.

181.   There will also be situations where adequate coverage was
provided on this topic in the pre-feasibility report. In these cases no
further mention is needed in the feasibility report, provided all
readers have access to the pre-feasibility report.

III. STRATEGIC PLAN FOR WATER SUPPLY AND SANITATION

182.   The aim of this chapter is to select the preferred project for
development in the near term in the context of the recommended strategy
for developing the water supply and sanitation systems throughout the
planning period. As with the description of the project area and the
need for a project, the discussion on the strategic plan for sector
services within the project area should be more or less complete in the
pre-feasibility report (paras. 98-140).

183.   Information and analyses which were not available at the time
of the pre-feasibility report should be highlighted. Either the
previous strategic plan for water and sanitation should be confirmed or
a revised strategic plan should be presented. In either case the
summary information should include:

-- the planning period and project objectives;

-- service coverage and service standards considered and selected for water supply and sanitation services;

-- primary health care and other programs affecting the impact of water supply and sanitation services;

-- community preferences and affordability;

-- quantification of future demands for services;

-- a screening and ranking of alternative projects;

-- recommended development plan for water supply and sanitation systems throughout the planning period;

-- costs of implementing the strategic plan.

IV. THE PROPOSED PROJECT

184.   This chapter describes the recommended project in detail. Information presented here is based on extensive analyses and preliminary design. Summary information in the report is supported in back-up documentation in annexes.

Objectives

185.   Project objectives should be expressed in two ways. General development objectives should include estimates of:

-- health improvements;

-- reduced burden in carrying water and expected impact, particularly on women and children (released time and energy);

-- improved living standards;

-- pollution abatement;

-- staff development;

-- institutional improvements.

Another possible general objective for the project is to be used as a model for replication by similar projects elsewhere in the country.

186.   Operational objectives for the project concern improvements in service coverage and standards for water supply and sanitation systems. Each objective should be quantified (to the extent practicable), and a schedule for achieving these objectives presented. Specific reference should be made to the target groups which the project will serve.

> NOTE: Future evaluation of the project will measure its results in terms of this original statement of objectives. This provides further rationale for developing realistic objectives.

Project Users and Their Perspectives

187.   Define by number and location the people (and, if appropriate, the institutions) who will benefit from the project. This estimate of project beneficiaries should be realistic, taking into account probable constraints on the acceptance and use of project services.

188.   Indicate which people in the project area will not benefit from the project and explain why they will not have access to improved services after the project is implemented.

NOTE: Longer term solutions for serving these people should also be given.

189.   Explain the selection, role, involvement and input of potential users of the project in the planning process. Explain what plans exist to involve project users in helping to construct the project and eventually operating it.

NOTE: The role of women as active participants in project planning and execution should be explicitly considered as they are frequently "manager" of water and sanitation services at the household level. Women should be involved in gathering and analyzing data about project users.

Rehabilitation of Existing Water Supply and Sanitation Systems

190.   Explain any proposals to rehabilitate and improve existing sector facilities. Explain why existing facilities need to be rehabilitated and discuss what plans have been formulated to ensure that the proposed project systems will not themselves fall into disuse.

NOTE: Opportunities for system rehabilitation should have been discovered earlier in the planning process (paras. 97 and 130) so the feasibility report ought to be able to refer to activities already underway.

191.   Explain and justify any proposed abandonment of existing water supply and sanitation facilities.

Project Description

192.   Define the project in the context of the strategic plan through which it was selected. Explain the priority of the recommended project.

193.   Outline all the components of the proposed project, with maps, photos and drawings as appropriate. Summarize information for presentation in the report and provide more detailed information in annexes.

NOTE: Water supply and sanitation components of the project should be described separately with the emphasis depending on whether or not both services are covered in the project.

194.   For the water supply and sanitation facilities, describe in detail:

-- the role, location, design criteria, number and capacity of each component;

-- the performance specifications, technical description (dimensions, materials, etc.), and method of construction of each component;

-- the status of the design and degree of preparation of each component;

-- any consulting services required to attain the objectives of the project;

-- whether and how components to be located in houses and yards, such as water and wastewater service pipes and plumbing, are included. If these essential components are not included, then estimate their cost and explain how they will be financed and built.

195.   For the supporting activities, rationalize and describe in detail:

-- components to strengthen the performance of sector agencies (such as staff training and improved bill collection and accounting systems). Specify the numbers of people involved, achievement targets, the timing of programs, responsibilities for their completion, and so on;

-- components for other project participants e.g. training of contractors, extension workers and project users. Again, specify precisely what is to be done, when, by which agencies, the personnel required, how the community is to be involved, and how this is to be coorinated with construction.

Integration of the Project with Existing and Future Systems

196.   Explain how the various physical components will be integrated into the existing water and sanitation systems. Also explain how proposed supporting activities (such as staff development) relate to the existing and future delivery systems, and how communities to be served will be involved in planning, construction and operation of facilities.

197.   Discuss system developments planned to follow the project and the physical relationships between the project and future system facilities. Explain how other projects will be prepared to meet future needs after the proposed project is operational.

Responsibilities for Project Implementation

198.   This section describes how the project will be designed and built and how it will later be operated and maintained. First explain the implementation phase, including related matters.

-- Explain the future operating agency's role during implementation and the procedure by which it will take over operational responsibility if another agency is responsible for implementing the project;

-- Identify all government agencies involved in project implementation and describe the role of each. Designate the lead agency to manage implementation of the project and outline proposed arrangements to coordinate all inputs;

-- Describe all non-government organizations such as health committees, cooperatives, tenants' associations and women's groups which might serve as focal points for motivating and mobilizing community involvement in the project. Outline their potential roles;

-- Specify the roles of any necessary consultants. Define their tasks, including terms of reference, level of effort and present status of each task. Consider whether foreign consultants are needed;

-- Describe the expected role of local and foreign suppliers and contractors in project construction and the role of staff of public agencies (force account) and non-government organizations;

-- Estimate the numbers and types of workers required to construct the project and compare these human resource requirements to the workforce available locally and nationally, in the light of other major construction activities foreseen during the project period;

-- Describe procurement procedures and regulations both for components financed by local and external funds, including the normal amount of time it takes to approve tender documents, award contracts, and take delivery;

-- Explain any special procurement procedures required or proposed for project implementation;

-- List materials to be imported, explain necessary procedures to acquire them and estimate delivery periods;

-- Outline equipment and material standards and explain any variations between local and relevant international standards;

-- Outline all legislative and administrative approvals required to implement the various project components. Particularly refer to water rights (for water supply projects); water quality criteria (government regulations covering outputs from water treatment and waste treatment plants); land required for project facilities; and possible changes in building regulations and codes;

-- Discuss present and proposed responsibilities and arrangements for preparing detailed plans to expand water supply and waste disposal facilities after the project becomes operational.

Cost Estimates

199.   Provide a summary of the estimated cost of the entire project and detailed cost estimates for each project component for each year of the project construction period. This summary requires the consideration and discussion of many related factors:

-- Make realistic provision for unexpected costs (physical contingencies) for each component;

NOTE: Items with greater uncertainty (for example, tunnels or deep wells to be located where the geology is not fully known) should have greater contingencies.

-- Estimate base prices for each element (at a specified time) for each year of implementation before applying an allowance for price increases (inflation) in the future;

-- Provide a summary of expected annual costs to show the estimated cash flow requirements for the project;

-- Break down costs into foreign exchange and local currency components and explain the basis of the breakdown;

-- Explain fully how the costs were estimated and list all basic assumptions, particularly those for unit prices, physical contingencies and price increases;

-- Compare the cost estimates for the proposed project with those for recent similar or related projects in the region or country.

Implementation Schedule

200.   Provide a detailed and realistic implementation schedule for all project components, complete with a graphical summary. Depict the tasks of each group involved, with activities illustrated logically according to implementation plans.

201.   If assistance is required from consultants, make allowances for all activities including:

-- determination of the short list;

-- preparation and review of terms of reference;

-- preparation of proposals by consultants;

-- review of proposals;

-- contract negotiations and approval;

-- mobilization;

-- execution and completion of assignment.

202.   For physical components, show allowances for all activities, including:

-- preparation of final designs;

-- preparation and review of draft tender documents;

-- bidding by contractors;

-- review of bids;

-- contract negotiations and approval;

-- mobilization;

-- construction;

-- commissioning and initial operation;

-- final completion date.

NOTE: Where self-help activities are planned, allow for seasonal variations in the availability of local labor, and the time required for community consultation and mobilization.

203.   Describe the implementation schedule for supporting activites (such as community consultation, staff training, promotion and education) in relation to the project objectives and physical components. Focus on the human resources development program, particularly the advance training of local staff needed for project commissioning and initial operation and maintenance.

204.   Ascertain critical steps logically and list them separately. Include administrative steps such as the provision of the required budget, land acquisition and approval for water abstraction as well as conventional steps related to recruitment of consultants and bidding and award of contracts. This can be facilitated by the use of critical path analysis.

205.   The proposed project for which financial assistance is being sought may exclude some components of a comprehensive development program. For example, urban upgrading may be under a separate agency and, for administrative reasons, may not be included in the defined project. Define and clearly describe, to the extent possible, cost estimates of all such complementary inputs and make definite proposals with regard to how and when the funds are to be provided, and how these efforts are to be organized and linked.

Future Operation and Maintenance of the Project

206.   — Describe all groups (government and non-government) which
         will be involved in operation and maintenance after the
         project facilities are built.

       -- Estimate the total financial resources required each year
          to operate and maintain the project, bearing in mind the
          need to replace various components as they are broken or
          worn out.

       -- Define all responsibilities, estimate the inputs required
          from each group (in terms of staff, equipment and
          materials) and explain the arrangements for coordinating
          the activities of the groups involved.

       -- Describe, in particular, how any "self-help" community
          operation and maintenance is to be organized, what
          technical assistance will be provided, by whom and under
          what conditions. Consider also the role of women in
          operation and maintenance, both community wide and at the
          household level.

       -- Estimate annual costs, by each group, for future
          operation and maintenance with variations according to
          output levels and factors) such as expected requirements
          for personnel, energy, chemicals, and transport. Also
          note expected increases in "current" prices of major
          items.

       -- Assess the project's energy requirements and indicate how
          these can be reliably supplied.

       -- Outline existing or proposed operating regulations,
          by-laws and ordinances relevant to the project.

       -- Present proposals for monitoring and evaluating project
          effectiveness against original objectives, including
          monitoring criteria and the type of reports expected to
          be submitted.

National Industrial Capability

207.   — Describe the capability of local industries to supply the
         materials needed to build and operate the project.

       -- Review the capability of national contractors to build
          the various components of the project.

-- Discuss possible ways of improving the capabilities of local industries and contractors to participate in the project.

-- Explain whether supply and contracting capabilities have influenced the design of the project.

-- Describe the way in which materials required to construct the project facilities are moved within the country from their places of origin (local factories for domestic goods or ports for imported goods) to the project sites. Explain any transportation, administrative or other possible constraints likely to affect project implementation.

Environmental Impacts

208.   Briefly describe the various environmental impacts which are expected to result from the project, including those on public health and or water, air and land resources. For each impact discuss proposals to reduce adverse impacts and increase positive impacts through project design and operation. Distinguish between temporary or short-term impacts associated with project construction and longer-term impacts of project operation.

209.   Provide a general prognosis of changes in <u>public health</u> expected to result from the project.

-- Where data permit, include a list of diseases related to water supply and sanitation, including present morbidity and mortality rates and outline the improvements expected to occur after the project becomes operational;

-- Explain qualitatively the probable consequences of expected improvements in health. Indicate time and energy savings for women and children. Describe anticipated improvements in nutrition from use of extra water or wastewater in domestic agriculture, i.e. vegetables, fruits, poultry and pigs;

-- Outline possible negative impacts, such as the risk of introducing schistosomiasis, or spreading malaria by creating reservoirs or increasing stagnant water in residential areas if drainage and sewerage improvements do not keep up with increases in the supply of water.

210.   Examine possible impacts on <u>water resources</u> for the water supply component.

-- Analyze the effect of withdrawing water from the surface
   or groundwater sources;

-- Estimate the reliability of the water source,
   particularly in drought conditions, bearing in mind
   probable future developments and especially major water
   uses such as irrigation;

-- Outline plans for disposal of any wastes (such as water
   used for filter and backwash and sludge from
   sedimentation tanks) during water treatment processes.

211.   Similarly examine possible water resources impacts for the
sanitation component.

-- Estimate the impact on local surface water resources of
   disposal systems which discharge to the nearest water
   course such as a stream, river or lake;

-- Consider impacts on local groundwater of on-site
   sanitation systems;

-- Evaluate existing drainage arrangements when these have
   to handle increased quantities of sullage water and
   consider all appropriate reuse possibilities;

-- For disposal systems which include treatment, assess
   treatment proposals, effluent quality and quantity, and
   the probable impact on the receiving water;

-- Discuss the prospects for improved water resources
   management, for example, flood control, low flow
   augmentation and water reuse.

V. INSTITUTIONAL AND FINANCIAL ASPECTS

212.   This chapter describes how the proposed project will be
implemented and how it will be subsequently operated and maintained. A
clear definition of every organization involved in all aspects of
project implementation (detail design, construction and commissioning)
should have been provided in the previous chapter, along with the
proposed arrangements for coordinating all inputs.

213.   In the long term, project benefits depend at least as much on
the organization(s) responsible for operating and maintaining the
project as they do on the organization which constructs it. Sometimes
the same organizations are involved in both stages. Where separate

entities are involved in construction and operation and maintenance, explain detailed arrangements for a smooth transition from the construction stage to the operational stage.

NOTE: Generally speaking, financing agencies require more information on the financial and management systems of agencies responsible for large infrastructure projects, particularly those producing substantial revenue, than for smaller projects which provide water and sanitation facilities as more of a service than a utility operation. In all cases, however, it is necessary to show that institutions already (or will soon) exist which are capable of developing and operating the project effectively to meet its basic objectives. It is also necessary to demonstrate that all proposed loans can be repaid.

Organization and Management

214.   Describe the existing and proposed organizations which will build and later operate and maintain the existing and expanded water supply and sanitation systems. For each organization the following variables should be considered:

-- management activities, including strategic planning; tactical planning and management control; operational planning and control; and respective management levels in the agency;

-- organizational functions or systems;

-- decision-making processes and the management information systems that support them.

215.   In discussing the various organizations the main points should be summarized in the the report but more detailed information can be presented in supporting annexes. Topics to be discussed include:

-- historical development and responsibilities of the entity;

-- legal basis and possible legal constraints (attach relevant legislation);

-- organization charts, existing and proposed;

-- the relationship within each organization between different functional groups (planning, design, construction, operations, finance, etc.) and between different regional offices for geographically dispersed organizations;

-- external relationships with government agencies or other organizations involved in sector activities (engineering, public health, environment, procurement, etc.);

-- the process for developing policies and making major decisions.

216.   Pay particular attention to those organizations responsible for supporting activities (such as promotion and education) which are expected to proceed along with the operation of physical facilities for water supply and sanitation facilities. The role of theseorganizations and of possible related groups (social workers, local cooperatives, women's groups, extension workers, etc.) should be carefully examined. Make appropriate recommendations for strengthening these organizations and providing adequate staff.

217.   The basic task of the agency which will operate the facilities provided under the project is to provide water supply and/or sanitation services to people in the project area. This places particular importance on the consumer relations of the organization and communications with the users of these services. Describe the organization's system and procedures for:

-- determining consumer needs and preferences for water supply and sanitation services and establishing priorities for meeting basic needs on an equitable basis;

-- encouraging acceptance of new services and technologies;

-- conducting a public information program to explain services, policies, reduction of wastage, and charging practices;

-- extending services to new consumers;

-- local monitoring of services and arranging for repairs;

-- settling complaints.

218.   Review the various management systems of the organization which will operate the facilities provided under the project, along with proposed changes, and discuss:

-- how budgets for capital and recurrent expenditures and for revenues will be prepared and approved;

-- accounting systems for expenditures and for revenues;
    their relationship to budgets; control systems (including
    spending authorizations and payment procedures) and
    monitoring and reporting procedures;

-- internal and external audit responsibilities and
    procedures;

-- maintenance programs, procedures, facilities and records;

NOTE: Distinguish preventive maintenance (that is,
      maintenance planned in advance) from repairs which
      take place after equipment breaks down (crisis
      response);

-- vehicle control and operation for the entire
    organization;

-- purchasing and storekeeping of materials and equipment.

Staffing Implications and Training

219.   The quality of the operating organization depends primarily on
its employees. This section should assess the present situation in
terms of management and personnel.

-- Explain the chief constraints on effective management
    from the view of managers at various levels, with
    recommendations for minimizing these constraints;

-- Summarize the positions and actual staff (permanent and
    temporary) broken down according to occupational
    categories and geographic location in accordance with the
    organization chart;

-- Comment on the number and quality of staff in each
    category;

-- Explain the ratio of staff employed to the number of
    people served;

-- Compare staffing levels with similar agencies in the same
    country and discuss any major differences;

-- Explain the policies and practices of the agency in using
    either the private sector or other public sector
    organizations to provide personnel assistance
    (consultants or contractors);

-- Indicate the salary ranges for all staff levels and compare these with other public sector employees;

-- Comment on the capability of the agency to attract and retain new staff and discuss the conditions of employment, career prospects and job satisfaction as perceived by staff at various levels; and

-- Provide data on recruitment of new staff and turnover of existing staff in recent years, and comment on any problems.

220.   Future staffing and training plans for each organization involved in project operations merit special attention.

-- Comment on the possibility of assigning some tasks to staff in other agencies;

-- Make projections of probable staff needs, by categories over the next five years, to reach the project objectives;

-- Compare future staff requirements to the available situation and define the potential shortfall (if any);

-- Review government and agency policies for personnel development within the water supply and sanitation sector;

-- Assess all programs for training and upgrading staff used by each agency. Include data on numbers involved in each of the past five years. Distinguish between formal training programs and on-the-job training. Comment on the location of various staff groups with respect to the training opportunities;

-- Describe other training programs available throughout the country (such as at high schools, technical colleges, universities, training centers and other public agencies). Also explore the possible use of foreign advisers, secondment of staff to other organizations, study tours, workshop, seminars, etc;

-- Comment on the possible and actual use of training programs outside the country by the agencies;

-- Outline agency plans to recruit required staff in the future and to provide appropriate staff motivation, training and retraining;

-- Comment on possible assistance required from the government or other sources to implement suitable training programs;

-- Describe and comment on training programs for field workers in related programs such as agricultural extension, primary health care, and nutrition;

-- Discuss the possible need to retrain and employ people who may lose their jobs because of the project (water vendors, night soil collectors, etc.);

-- Summarize training proposals by skill category and by training methods for future years, making appropriate allowance for turnover so that the supply of human resources equals or exceeds the total projected requirement.

Financial History of Operating Organization

221.   Describe existing accounting and financial control systems and records of the organization proposed to operate the project facilities.

NOTE: Where possible, present standard financial statements (income statements, balance sheets and cash flows) for each of the past five years. These statements can be placed in annexes but the results need to be summarized in the report.

-- Describe any financial objectives of the organization;

-- Explain the process by which physical assets are formally acquired and valued by the organization;

-- Explain depreciation methods and procedures for abandoning obsolete facilities;

-- Discuss the overall financial position of the organization (past and present) and explain the major expenditures and sources of operating income;

-- Summarize the financial health of the organization (past and present);

-- In inflationary situations, assess the value of the assets and the resulting financial situation in real terms;

-- Discuss any financial problems, including their impact on operations and performance and therefore on services provided to the public;

-- Discuss alternative remedies;

-- Outline any constraints imposed on the organization's financial position by factors outside management's control e.g. need for government approval of tariffs, pay scales, etc.

Charges for Services

222.   This section reviews past charges, describes the process and policy concerning future charges and compares projected future charges with marginal costs.

-- Explain the objectives used to establish tariffs for the services provided by the operating organzation;

-- Outline actual tariffs for all services for each of the past five years and comment on any changes;

-- Outline all steps which were followed in obtaining approval to the most recent change;

-- Comment on the practicality of cross-subsidizing the poverty group by industrial, commercial, institutional and more affluent consumers within the project area and of subsidizing more expensive schemes with revenues from less expensive ones;

-- Outline any established or proposed policies for past and future revenues, particularly for services which will be provided by the project. Specifically examine the desirability of step tariffs;

-- Estimate the effect of charging for services on residents of various income levels in the project area, to determine affordability of tariffs;

-- Compare future to present tariffs and comment on the practicality of obtaining approval to the necessary changes;

-- Compare the proposed tariff structure with the estimated long run marginal costs of providing service improvements;

-- Summarize expected tariffs and revenues in future years;

-- Explain the organization's recourse if consumers do not
   pay charges.

Future Financial Situation

223.   Prepare annual financial statements (income statements,
balance sheets and cash flows) for the project operating entity. The
statements are normally prepared to cover up to three years after the
proposed project is operational, but this period may be extended
depending upon particular financing arrangements.

-- State explicitly all basic assumptions for the financial
   forecasts, including the assumed terms and conditions of
   all financial sources;

-- Discuss any interesting or unusual features of these
   projections;

-- Demonstrate the future financial health of the
   organization, particularly its ability to cover all
   operating and maintenance expenditures. Also examine its
   ability to generate a portion of its future capital
   requiements from revenues;

-- Estimate the organization's rate of return on net fixed
   assets;

-- State the internal financial rate of return of the
   project, using incremental net revenues and project
   costs.   (This may not be appropriate with small
   projects).

Financing Plan

224.   This section summarizes all sources of funds for the
implementation of the project. The overall financial situation for all
programs of the responsible organization should be examined, as well as
the financing plan for the specific project.

-- Identify possible sources and terms of finance (internal
   and external) to meet the total cost of the project and
   prepare year-by-year estimates of cash flows for the
   organizations implementing the project;

-- Explain whether interest during construction is included
   in the financing plan and why;

-- Explain carefully the procedures that are involved and the sequence followed to obtain the funds required for implementation of the project.

225.   International financial agencies do not participate in projects where accountability is in doubt. They normally require, at a minimum, that an accounting and reporting system, capable of reporting all project transactions accurately and promptly, will be operational from the start of project implementation. Hence this section needs to discuss appropriate arrangements for future accounting and reporting. Existing and proposed arrangements for auditing the organization's accounts should also be explained.

VI. CONCLUSIONS AND RECOMMENDATIONS

226.   This chapter states whether the proposed project is feasible when judged from all perspectives and recommends actions to be taken for its implementation. It also discusses issues and risks associated with project implementation.

Justification

227.   Discuss in qualitative terms why the proposed project is justified and should proceed.

-- Summarize how the project will satisfy the objectives and confirm that the proposed project is the most cost-effective solution to meeting these objectives;

-- Explain the interest of the intended users of the project and their role (past and proposed) in project preparation. Make specific reference to the willingness and capability of the intended beneficiaries to support the project, including the payment of charges for services;

-- If project benefits can be reasonably quantified and valued, compare them to project costs for each year in the future. (In many projects, mainly because of the lack of data, it is not possible to determine the benefits in quantitative terms.);

-- Discuss the effect of not proceeding with the project.

Conclusions

228.   Summarize briefly the conclusions which demonstrate that the project is feasible:

-- economically;

-- technically;

-- financially;

-- socially and culturally;

-- environmentally;

-- institutionally.

Issues and Risks

229.   Identify all issues which may pose a risk to project implementation and operation. Make a judgment as to the gravity of each risk and suggest ways of minimizing such risks.

Uncertainties and Sensitivities

230.   Examine the consequences of small and large changes in the major assumptions on which the report is based. Test the sensitivity of the project to changes in basic parameters such as:

-- delay in project implementation;

-- reduction in benefits;

-- delay in tariff increases;

-- increases in cost;

-- changes in demand.

Recommended Actions

231.   List the key actions which need to be taken in order to approve, implement and operate the project successfully. Include any policy questions which need to be resolved.

-- Each recommendation should name the agency or individual to be responsible for the action with a suggested timetable;

-- Provide an outline scope of work where detailed activities need to be undertaken (such as future assignments by consultants or fundamental institutional improvements);

-- Emphasize potential difficulties which could critically delay project progress.

232. Indicate specific actions which the agency responsible for project implementation can commence so as to avoid delays while necessary agreements are reached on project approval and financing.

E. GUIDELINE FOR RURAL WATER SUPPLY AND SANITATION PROGRAM

Table of Contents

E. GUIDELINE FOR RURAL WATER SUPPLY AND SANITATION PROGRAM

BASIC PRINCIPLES

Background

233.   The Identification, Pre-Feasibility and Feasibility Report Guidelines of the Project Preparation Handbook can be used in the preparation of any water supply and sanitation project. These Guidelines are comprehensive enough to satisfy requirements of complex and large projects serving metropolitan areas, large cities and towns. Their use for rural projects would require considerable judgement in the determination of what to include or exclude. As a consequence, this simplified Guideline has been prepared for the preparation of simpler programs in rural areas. Another reason for preparing this Guideline is to emphasize some of the special considerations involving rural projects, such as the need to stress community involvement in the planning, implementation and operation of facilities, the special requirements imposed on institutions supporting rural projects, and other aspects briefly discussed below.

234.   Definitions of "urban" and "rural" differ greatly throughout the world. Rural communities range from thousands of people in towns, through scattered, separate farmhouses, to nomads who stay put for only a few weeks or months at a time. In some countries the definition of rural communities is based on the size of population, in some on political divisions, and in others on the lack of public facilities.

235.   Rural water supply and sanitation programs usually consist of many sub-projects providing for the planning, construction and placing into operation of a large number of facilities in numerous locations over a large area, in a stated period of time. They also provide for community development, health and hygiene education, training, technical assistance and operation and maintenance support.

Objectives

236.   The main objective of rural water supply is to provide safe water, easily accessible, in quantities adequate for drinking, food preparation, personal hygiene, and sometimes small livestock, at a cost in keeping with the economic level of the communities and through facilities which can be easily operated and maintained at the local level. The objective of the sanitation component is to provide means for the safe disposal of human excreta through low-cost, easily-maintained facilities, thus completing the effort to protect the health of the people from water and excreta-related diseases.

237.   The facilities to be installed should be appropriate to the local conditions and acceptable to the users. Improvements in water supply can start with the protection and improvement of traditional sources, the installation of handpumps, piping water to central public water points (standpipe) and finally piping of water to yards and houses (house connection). To break the chain of transmission of certain diseases, improved excreta disposal methods must be provided along with improved water supplies. For a rural area the latrine, properly located, constructed and maintained, will be an adequate facility. There are many types of latrines, ranging from a simple borehole to a more complex pour-flush type with a water seal.[1]

Program Planning

238.   As a rule, a rural water supply and sanitation program consists of several, often many sub-projects. These sub-projects may serve individual villages, groups of villages, rural towns, and dispersed populations in a defined area. Frequently, a program is a portion (time-slice) of a provincial, state or national sector program which may include both rural and urban projects.

239.   One significant difference between an individual project and a program is that the former is well defined prior to implementation while the latter consists of planning and implementing a large number of projects simultaneously, i.e. while some projects are being constructed, others are being planned. The program budget is therefore established on the basis of relatively detailed information about a time-slice of the program, for example the sub-projects planned for implementation during the first year, and less detailed information, such as the number of people and villages, about individual schemes to be implemented during the later years of the program. Average unit costs derived from the first time-slice and similar programs are used to estimate total costs for the population to be served by the entire program. As more detailed information becomes available during program implementation, the area and population may be increased or may need to be reduced for the program to remain within the original budget. Successful implementation of such a program requires:

> -- a national or regional agency (existing or being created with technical assistance), that can competently plan and manage the development of each individual sub-project within a comprehensive program;

---

[1]   See " Appropriate Technology for Water Supply and Sanitation: A Summary of Technical and Economic Options: Summary Report"; J.M. Kalbermatten, D.S. Julius and C.G. Gunnerson. See Bibliography.

-- criteria for determining priorities within the sector and for providing that the most important sub-projects are implemented first (sub-project selection criteria);

-- the national or regional agency to have proven experience in the preparation and execution of similar sub-projects, in accordance with agreed upon standards and criteria (or can be provided with the necessary technical assistance);

-- the agency to be sufficiently decentralized to provide effective technical assistance to entities implementing and operating sub-projects and to monitor their activities, or to implement and operate sub-projects if required to do so.

240.   The program planning process may be initiated by government planners (5 year plans, regional development plans, sector programs, etc.) or by community or non-government organizations active in promoting rural development. The project data sheet (Annex 2) is a convenient method of providing the initially required information to get the necessary approvals to start the process. An identification report may not be required, especially if institutions involved are already experienced in rural program planning or the program is part of an existing long range development plan. The responsible authorities would select an agency to plan the program, usually the same organization which will be responsible to undertake or oversee implementation and operation. The preparation process would then generally take place according to the following steps:

-- data collection;

-- establishing the need for the program;

-- definition of program objectives;

-- development of:

    o sub-project selection criteria,

    o sub-project design criteria,

    o methods of construction;

-- preparation of standard designs;

-- development of financial and cost recovery policies;

NOTE: If criteria and policies already exist at the national or regional level, this task would consist of a review leading to recommendations to accept or modify existing criteria and policies. Frequently, many government and non-government (voluntary) organizations, all using their own criteria and equipment preferences, work in a country's rural areas. A review should attempt to identify the most effective criteria and to coordinate a more widespread use of the best.

-- preliminary design, fieldwork and initial consultation with users/communities;

-- formulation of proposals for:

    o institutional arrangements and technical support to community for sub-project implementation and maintenance,

    o training of agency and local staff (village caretaker),

    o support activities such as health education,

    o financing and cost recovery;

-- agreement on proposals (with or without modifications) by appropriate authorities (for example, planning and budget office, responsible ministry, agencies providing support activities, etc.);

-- selection and preparation of sub-projects to be implemented during the first year of the program;

-- tentative agreement on implementation, maintenance and financing with communities included in first year program;

-- preparation and submittal of documentation to approval authorities;

-- approval of program by appropriate authorities on basis of criteria, agreements and first year sub-projects;

-- agreement with communities concerning the initiation of sub-project implementation and training activities;

-- preparation and implementation of sub-projects for subsequent years in program period;

-- monitoring and feedback into the program development and sub-project preparation process.

241.   The selection of sub-projects follows a screening process which considers, successively, various indicators reflecting need and costs to establish an order of priority for project implementation. This ranking ensures that those communities with most urgent needs (most serious health problems, greatest scarcity of water) and/or those able to serve the greatest number of people at lowest costs and/or greatest capacity or willingness for self help and maintenance, will be served first.   The selection criteria are not mutually exclusive and the process requires subjective judgements, especially when there are insufficient funds to permit implementation of sub-projects for all villages in a program area.   In such a case, a weighting of selection criteria, which will result in a clear ranking in order of priority, acceptable to approval authorities, is helpful.   Sub-projects would then be executed in the order of priority established by this ranking.

242.   The first step in this ranking process is to determine the need for each sub-project.   The need could be based on such aspects as the existence of a serious health problem from water-related diseases, the burden of obtaining water from long distances or great depths, seasonal shortages of water for livestock, and the negative health impact due to the absence of sanitation facilities.   Other criteria could include the possibility of productive enterprise if water were available, for example, for small scale food processing.

243.   The second step is to investigate whether the sub-project is the least costly means of meeting the needs of the community.   The type of facilities to be provided should be appropriate to the local situation and customs.   The alternatives to be compared may vary from point sources of supply such as springs and wells with handpumps, to more complete systems with a protected source, transmission line and basic distribution network with standpipes and house connections. Sanitation facilities will generally be on-site systems.   The assessment of costs should include the capital and operating costs at the local level.

244.   The third step is to determine whether the community has the technical and financial capacity, as well as the social-administrative structure, to operate and manage the system and has expressed the willingness to do so. (The second and third steps are closely related and should, in fact, be considered together.)   The final step is to list the sub-projects in order of the ranking derived from the weighted criteria.

245   Among the criteria which can be used for establishing an order of priority for sub-project selection for implementation are the following:

      -- existence (or creation) of a village organization to
         implement, operate and maintain facilities;

-- interest of the villagers (request for assistance, willingness to contribute to capital and operation and maintenance costs);

-- seriousness of the situation with respect to water-related disease as compared with other villages;

-- possible reductions in the present costs of obtaining water (reduction in carrying distance);

-- poor water quality and seasonal variation in existing sources (fluorides, dry season);

-- potential for future economic development;

-- availability of support services such as personal hygiene training;

-- size of settlement;

-- accessibility of village for constructing and supervising village water supply;

-- grouping of villages to provide most efficient solution (less travel for contractors or support personnel, single source for several villages, etc.);

-- per family or per capita cost of proposed facilities (least investment serving greatest number).

246.   Normally, the program agency and development finance institution would reach agreement on sub-project selection and design criteria. Following such agreement, a sample of sub-projects would be prepared and reviewed. The other sub-projects in the program would then be prepared and implemented by the program agency, with only limited involvement by the external agency.

Financial Aspects

247.   In urban communities which have a wide range of consumers with different levels of income, it is possible through suitable rate structures to provide basic services to the poor at affordable prices, including subsidized tariffs, and still generate enough revenue to cover the operating costs and a portion of investments. The urban populations are usually concentrated and served by a single water and sewer system and organization.

248.   In rural communities which do not have such a wide range of income levels and are generally poor, experience has shown that it is often not possible for the communities to meet much more than operating

and maintenance costs. The villages are usually scattered and must be served by numerous wells, individual, or regional systems. Support from outside the village will be required for major repairs and advice on operation and maintenance, even if the village operates the system. In the systems where only standpipes or handpumps are installed, it is very difficult to obtain more than a token payment, which may not be sufficient for operation and maintenance. The cost and the means of financing this support should be carefully evaluated in the project design and in the determination of the size of the project. Failure to provide for maintenance on a continuing basis will result in a gradual breakdown of the facilities and their eventual abandonment. Sanitation systems usually consist of on-site facilities which can be built and maintained by the owner, usually with some technical assistance and the provision of some material (squat plate, etc.).

249.   The systems to be built should represent the least-cost solution. The villagers should participate in the selection process and contribute to the construction of the system by providing land, local materials, unskilled labor, or cash. Experience has shown that they usually are able to contribute about 10%-20% of the cost of the system. Important prerequisites are the desire of the particular village to have a water supply system, participation in the selection and design of the system and in its construction and operation, and willingness to pay for the service once in operation. The method of charging and collecting may largely determine the effectiveness of cost recovery. Payment to a local caretaker could be in kind, money for spare parts could be collected at harvest time, or small payments could be collected on market days.

Technical Aspects

250.   The following discussion highlights some technical issues specific to or particularly important in rural water supply and sanitation programs.

i) Sources of Water

251.   The best source of water is one that is safe without treatment and can be delivered by gravity and, failing this, by pumping and is located within a reasonable distance. Groundwater is generally of better quality than surface water and, in fortunate circumstances, it is found in springs that can be protected and used directly. Where surface water treatment is necessary, simple processes should be employed to permit village operation of the facilities. Roofwater catchment schemes similarly need to provide for simple water quality protection measures to eliminate contamination from initial runoffs.

252.   After such preferred sources have been fully developed or where they are not available, it is necessary to develop other sources. In most areas where rural projects are to be developed, the knowledge of groundwater is limited or groundwater is considered to be scarce. However, the quantities required for basic human needs are not too great so that the possibility of using groundwater sources should always be investigated.

253.   Ideally, groundwater exploration and even test well drilling should have been carried out in the program area before the start of planning the program (at least for those sub-projects to be included in the first year program). Without adequate exploration, delays occur or expensive (due to conveyance and treatment costs) but more obvious surface sources are used. Programs should include adequate provisions for exploring and developing sources on a reasonable schedule and under the supervision of qualified personnel.

ii) Handpumps

254.   Handpumps are and likely will remain for the foreseeable future the principal means of water supply in rural areas, especially for dispersed populations. Manufacturers in many countries produce handpumps. In addition, several foot-operated pumps have been developed and are undergoing field trails. Some manufacturers offer expensive, allegedly longlasting pumps; others offer inexpensive, less durable models. The selection of the most appropriate pump remains a difficult problem, requiring technical and economic analyses.

255.   The problem is related to extremely heavy use, for which most of the earlier well-known makes were not designed, and lack of maintenance. Where pump installations are far apart and cannot be visited frequently, rugged and durable pumps are required; where pumps are easily accessible, it may be less expensive to have an intensive repair and replacement program. In any case, the cost of the handpump program should include not only the cost of the pumps and wells but the cost of supporting manpower, transportation, spare parts, and replacement equipment to maintain the pumps. The equipment and design should be standardized as far as possible.

iii) Wells

256.   One of the most frequently neglected details in the construction of wells is the finishing of the well, i.e., the platform and drainage facilities. Often, the well is not sealed against surface water infiltration, leading to contamination of the well water. The typical platforms and pump bases are usually too small and weak, designed for one-family use. Because these installations serve many people and there is constant drainage and spillage, platforms and the pump bases should be large, high and strong enough to resist heavy use, and sloped to drain away waste water so that pools of muddy water are

not formed through which people must walk and in which insects can
breed. Similar observations apply to standpipes, for which drainage
facilities are generally inadequate.

iv) House Connections and Standpipes

257.   In rural communities with limited water distribution systems
there will be more standpipes than house connections because such an
arrangement is the least expensive solution. The standpipes have
several drawbacks which can be overcome with motivation campaigns and
strong community participation. Standpipes can be damaged through
vandalism, can waste water through leaky or open faucets, or can cause
health hazards and nuisances because of inadequate drainage.
Furthermore, the people obtain only small amounts of water which can be
contaminated by dirty containers, transport to the house and improper
storage. It is also difficult to collect revenues from the users of
standpipes.

258.   More complete distribution systems with house connections are
more costly and account for about 50%-75% of the capital cost of the
water supply system. The cost depends primarily on the length of pipe
installed and secondarily on the diameter. Thus, it is possible to plan
the system to be expanded from mostly standpipes to house connections as
the community becomes more prosperous. Systems with house connections
make water more convenient and less liable to contamination. Collection
of revenues needed for maintenance is more effective from users with
house connections. In many countries, the responsible authorities have
assisted the villagers to install and finance the house connections,
with costs repaid over a period of time.

v) Sanitation

259.   Waterborne sewerage is usually too expensive for rural areas
and, any case, it requires larger quantities of water than can be
obtained from handpump or standpipe service.

260.   There are, however, several alternatives which provide
adequate means of excreta disposal. A properly located, constructed and
maintained latrine can meet all public health requirements. The latrine
can be a simple dry pit or borehole, a vault, or a wet type with pour-
flush discharge into a vault, septic tank or soakage pit.

261.   It is important to have a knowledge of local customs and
traditions so that a type of latrine acceptable to the beneficiaries can
be chosen. Unless proper use is made of the facility the desired
benefits will not be achieved. A knowledge of subsoil conditions is
also required to ensure technical feasibility and to avoid contamination
of underground aquifers. In general, the latrine should be of sturdy
construction and its design should allow easy and hygienic maintenance.
It is important to avoid the latrine becoming a breeding ground for

flies and mosquitoes, since this will defeat its basic objective of preventing the spread of disease. This, as well as the elimination of unpleasant odors often associated with private and communal latrines, can be achieved through the use of a properly designed, ventilated latrine.

vi) Standardization

262.   To simplify construction and maintenance and to permit bulk purchasing, standard equipment, materials and spare parts should be decided upon during the program preparation. Standard designs should be based upon such standard equipment and materials. All too frequently, water and sanitation systems are designed on a one-by-one basis and a multitude of different pipe sizes, materials, pumps and fittings result. It should be possible to reduce the type and size of materials and equipment to a small number and to establish standard designs. Construction of systems or parts that require special skills or knowledge, such as the drilling of wells, should normally be done by qualified contractors.

Socio-Cultural Aspects

263.   Water is not only needed for drinking and cooking but for personal hygiene. This means that water should be easily accessible; otherwise, the villagers may use other more convenient, but polluted sources. Sanitary disposal of human wastes is necessary to eliminate contamination of water and food and to prevent people from coming into direct contact with disease organisms. This is especially important in tropical areas where conditions favor the growth of many disease vectors. Sanitary facilities must be in keeping with local customs and habits, otherwise they will not be used.

264.   In many countries, it has been found that one of the principal causes of system failure has been the lack of participation of the villagers in every phase of the local water supply and sanitation schemes, and the lack of contribution to their construction and operation (in kind or cash). Unless users are involved from the beginning and are conscious of a need for safe water and sanitation, there is a danger that the facilities will not be properly used or maintained. To achieve full benefits from investments made, therefore, usually requires public health and hygiene education programs, tailored to local customs and beliefs.

265.   These programs should be carefully planned and adequately funded. They may be carried out by existing specialized institutions such as the Ministry of Health or by the staff of the agency in charge of water supply and sanitation. Each program should be directed to the users of the new facilities but should also include training of all water supply and sanitation personnel in the fundamentals of health and

hygiene education since they are in direct contact with the villagers and will continue to provide advice and support to them. The program should provide for staff, salaries, vehicles, equipment, materials, transport and other recurrent costs, as well as in-service training.

Institutional Aspects

266.   Organizations responsible at the national, regional, state and community levels for planning, execution and management are involved in rural water supply and sanitation programs. In many countries private non-governmental organizations are also carrying out such programs and their work should also reflect regional and national plans. Institutions responsible for health education and community development should also be involved. Coordination between these organizations and institutions, definition of their responsibilities, and appropriate financing arrangements are necessary. Access to involved agencies at the lowest level (district center) is generally more effective than coordination at headquarters. Where such access exists, the village or program agency then can call upon the agencies when needed.

267.   An organization capable of planning a rural water supply and sanitation program and preparing and executing sub-projects may exist or should be established. This agency should have a continuing source of funds, adequate and qualified staff, be able to prepare and monitor sub-projects and long-range programs, provide continuing support to the villages and act as the channel of communications with national/regional authorities.

268.   At the community level, the customary organization that deals with community works should be promoted and developed for assisting in the construction and maintenance of the facilities. In some countries, such an organization has taken the form of a local village committee, a cooperative, a special village water group, or some traditional body that represents the village. This organization should participate in the process of developing the local schemes. Non-governmental agencies working at the community level can play a valuable role in this community organization and development and help villages execute sub-projects.

Implementation and Management

269.   The planning and implementation of a water and sanitation program may be done by a combination of community participation, direct administration and contracts with consultants and contractors.

270.   The responsible agency should have or develop standard designs and selection criteria and a cost recovery policy. Enough hydrologic and hydrogeological information and investigation data should be

available to ensure that construction work can be started within a reasonable time. Sample designs should be available for about one year's work so that there will not be undue delay in project execution.

271. Arrangements should be made to have materials, supplies and equipment readily available before executing the agreement which formalizes village participation. Once the village has shown its willingness and desire to participate in the program, construction of the system should follow quickly. Too long a delay will destroy the credibility of the program.

272. The development and protection of spring supplies and infiltration galleries can be done by force account or contract if works are extensive. Very often the executing agency elects to purchase well-drilling equipment and do the work by force account. Experience indicates that the maintenance of such equipment has generally been poor and the rate of well-drilling has been low, both due to lack of adequately trained staff. It is often necessary to assist the executing agency with consultants in hydrogeology and well-drilling to train and supervise the well-drilling staff and/or contractors.

273. The construction of simple distribution systems and tanks can be done by the users, by contract and by force account. In all cases the villagers can provide unskilled labor, and usually also sand, gravel, stone or bricks.

274. The preferred solution in remote areas and for small systems should be construction by the villagers, assisted by the executing agency. Often the importation of a "foreman" with the necessary material is sufficient.

275. On-site sanitation facilities are usually constructed by the users after suitable instruction by the executing agency or the community health worker of the Ministry of Health. The executing agency generally provides some of the materials, such as the squat plate. Ministry of Health organizations in rural areas, even when well-staffed with personnel, often lack funds for travel and for carrying out health education programs. It is necessary to evaluate, in advance, the capacity of this ministry or alternative agencies for carrying out this part of the program.

Operation and Maintenance

276. One of the most serious problems is usually the poor maintenance of the systems once they have been built. For example, the record of handpump water supply programs is quite bad; failure rates of 30%-70% have been reported within two years after pump installations. Each time a system or handpump breaks down, the villagers will seek water elsewhere, often from unsafe and polluted sources.

277.   A rural water supply program should provide for continuing
technical and administrative support to the villages involved in the
program.   The method of support depends on the size of the area, the
number of villages and other considerations such as travel time.   Simple
systems of records and accounts and reporting should be developed,
whatever the support system,   so that suitable financial and management
information about the various systems is available to the supporting
agencies for performance monitoring.

278.   In some countries, a three tier system has been successfully
used.   At the first, or village, level, the villagers are responsible
for the degree of administration and maintenance that is within their
capability and specific individuals are trained and equipped to carry
out these tasks.   These individuals, often referred to as caretakers
(para. 249), are selected by the villagers.

279.   At a second level, located perhaps a day's journey away, is a
regional support office with a spare parts warehouse, and technicians to
make repairs with which the villagers cannot cope.   The regional office
technicians also visit the installations periodically to check on
routine maintenance and operation and see whether the installation is in
good repair.

280.   At a third level, the central office is responsible for
establishing policies and supervising and implementing the overall
program, budgeting, bulk purchase and supply of materials, and training
of second level personnel.   The importance of this system is that it
provides for village operation and support to the village.   The type of
organization which is appropriate for any specific program must reflect
local conditions in the program area.

281.   Whether the support mechanism selected is the described three
tier, a two tier or any other system, communications between the village
and the support organization are crucially important.   If a message
about a breakdown does not reach the support organization, help will
obviously not be forthcoming.   Eventually, regular visits, which should
be part of the support system, will discover the problem, but often too
late to prevent hardship.

Justification

282.   It is recognized that an adequate supply of safe water is
necessary for good health and productivity. Many studies have attempted
to quantify the health effects of improved water supply and sanitation.
For a variety of reasons no satisfactory method of quantifying these
benefits has so far been developed.   Thus, at the present state of
knowledge it is not possible to accurately or completely quantify
benefits.   Consequently, benefits should be quantified to the extent
possible and, in addition, a qualitative description should be provided
for those benefits which cannot be quantified.

REPORT FORMAT

Table of Contents

Page

EXECUTIVE SUMMARY

283.   The most important aspects of the report should be summarized for the convenience of individuals, particularly decision makers, who may not read the entire report. The summary should be written concisely and should include one or two simple location maps to present the proposed project clearly.

284.   The summary should tell:

-- program objectives,

-- work done,

-- conclusions, and

-- what action should be taken.

I.   INTRODUCTION

285.   This chapter briefly explains the reasons for the report and how it was prepared. It also provides background information about the water supply and sanitation sector.

Program Genesis

286.   -- Describe how the proposed program idea was developed.

-- Indicate who participated in the preparation of this report.

-- Make reference to related long-term plans for the sector, regional development, land use, water resources development, rural development, primary health care, etc.

II. THE WATER SUPPLY AND SANITATION SECTOR

287.   A brief description of the water supply and sanitation sector in the country should be presented, with emphasis on institutions active in rural areas, in particular the program area. Whenever government sector publications describe the sector sufficiently for a reader to gain a general understanding, this section can be eliminated, provided

reference is made to the relevant documentation. In that case, this information should be added to the INTRODUCTION and the sector chapter, detailed in paragraphs 288-293, eliminated.

288.   Broad information should be provided for the sector but specific discussions of the program area should normally be included in the next chapter rather than here. The principal entities in the sector, their relative activity and their programs should be briefly described. Some information about their size, personnel, areas of activity, competence and adequacy of funds should be provided, with an indication how this affects the proposed program.

Institutions

289.   -- Name and briefly describe government and non-government institutions which have an impact on:

   o water supply;
   o sanitation (excreta and wastewater disposal);
   o public health and health education.

   -- Provide detailed information on the institutions directly concerned with water supply and sanitation services including their:

   o purpose and goals;
   o operational responsibilities;
   o managerial capability;
   o staffing levels;
   o locations.

Population

290.   Countries have different definitions for rural communities: in some it is by population size (in some cases, under 2,000), in others by political jurisdiction, and still others by the availability of infrastructure.

   -- explain the criteria for defining the rural population;

   -- give the number of rural population living in communities, on farms;

   -- define income levels and standard of living and their regional variation.

Public Health

291.   Improvement of health is usually the principal objective of rural water supply and sanitation projects. Knowledge of existing health conditions is therefore important.

-- Cite public health indicators, such as life expectancy, morbidity and mortality of waterborne and water and sanitation related diseases;

-- Describe health services (curative and preventive);

-- Describe health education and hygiene training programs for rural areas and their:

    o   institutions,
    o   staffing and budget,
    o   community support requirements.

Water Resources and Control

292.   -- Provide an overview of available surface and groundwater resources.

-- Provide an overview of the meteorologic and hydrologic data available and comment on their reliability.

-- Indicate present and future water use trends and discuss any problems of water scarcity by regions.

Sector Policies

293.   Provide information about the national targets for service, financing, institutional development and related activities, such as community development. Describe:

-- service objectives;

-- financial policy for rural water supply and sanitation (user contribution, government support, funding of operation and maintenance);

-- community participation requirements in:

    o   system selection,
    o   construction,
    o   operation and maintenance,
    o   financing (capital as well as operation and maintenance);

-- arrangements for administrative and technical support.

NOTE: In many countries, experience has shown that, with a
well-organized community interested in having a water
supply system, it is possible to obtain a contribution in
labor and materials equivalent on the average to about
10%-20% of the construction cost. In addition, it is
possible to establish some system of rates and charges
that will pay for basic operation and maintenance or to
have the community assume responsibility for operation
and maintenance with government technical assistance.
Major repairs and technical assistance will need to be
furnished by the regional or national government, and the
funding of this is usually a government responsibility.

III. EXISTING CONDITIONS IN THE PROGRAM AREA

294.   This important chapter explains why a program is needed and
tells the reader about:

-- the program area and its people (villages and dispersed
population of a region);

-- the present water supply and sanitation services in the
program area;

-- the prospects for future development;

-- the need to improve existing services.

NOTE: It is particularly important to discuss the impact of the
program on other services. For example, water supply
projects often result in the need for major improvements
in sanitation. In practice the existing and future
standard for one service directly affects feasible
standards for another.[1] Even for minimum service, such
as handpumps or standpipes in rural areas, some provision

---

[1] For example, piped water supplies and house connections may
not be appropriate where population densities are high, soil
permeabilities low and sewers not affordable because the
wastewater which would result would actually aggravate public
health problems. Sewers, on the other hand, are not feasible
without an assured supply of piped water.

should be made for excreta and wastewater disposal. Discussion of plans for reuse or disposal should be a part of every report. Hence, the sanitation implications should be addressed even when the main focus of the report is a water supply sub-project. Technical details of systems not to be included in the proposed program need not be covered as extensively as technical details of services to be provided.

Program Area and Population

295. -- Describe the program area (refer to maps).

-- Give population distribution, indicate range of village size.

-- Provide a range of estimates for future population growth within the program area for the planning period and indicate the most probable growth rates.

-- Review and discuss any patterns of seasonal migration within the area.

Economic and Social Conditions

296. -- Give a general description of present living conditions for people of different socio-economic and ethnic groups.

-- Provide data on the number and location of residents in the program area according to income levels or other indicators of socio-economic status (if significant variations exist).

-- Analyze the health situation within the area, paying particular attention to diseases related to water and sanitation conditions. Discuss the most prevalent water- and sanitation-related diseases (including morbidity and mortality) in the project area and suggest how to control these. Also review the possible need for hygiene education.

-- Provide data on infant mortality and life expectancy and compare these to figures for other parts of the country.

-- Discuss status of relevant health care programs in the area as well as other projects (housing, rural development, etc.) with extension services which might relate to improvements in environmental sanitation.

-- Comment on local organizations, including women's clubs and informal groupings, which might become active participants in water supply and sanitation program implementation.

Regional Development Prospects

297. -- Give a brief description of the local economy and explain how the resource base affects residents of the region.

-- Comment on probable future development in the program area.

-- Discuss whether there are any linkages between improved sector services and general development prospects.

Sector Institutions

298. -- Discuss the role and responsibility of all institutions (government and non-government) involved in water supply and sanitation services in the program area. Also discuss institutions (public health agencies, regional planning agencies and community organizations) providing related services such as health, adult education, rural extension services, etc.

-- Explain statutory boundaries or other limits which affect these institutions and briefly review their past performance and assess the main constraints (political, financial, staff), if any, on their operations.

-- Comment on the effectiveness of cooperation among sector institutions in planning, building, operating and using water supply and sanitation services.

-- Describe cooperation among the beneficiary population and informal organizations (such as women's clubs, cooperatives, credit associations, irrigation associations, and volunteer organizations) which might be useful in sub-project implementation.

Available Water Resources

299. — Summarize the quantity and quality of surface and
groundwater resources, actual and potential, in the
program area and vicinity. Comment on the quality and
reliability of available data.

— Describe possible pollution problems which affect
available surface and groundwater resources.

— Summarize the role of various agencies in managing water
resources, particularly water allocation and water
quality control.

NOTE: Data and other background information should be presented
in annexes.

Existing Water Supply Services and Population Served

300.   This section should summarize and assess existing water supply
facilities (both public and private) in the program area. Describe them
briefly with a narrative of their development.

— pay particular attention to the operating and maintenance
status. Constraints on increasing services should be
highlighted.

NOTE: Use maps to delineate areas where facilities are located
and schematic diagrams, charts and tables of data to
summarize information. Additional background material
can be presented in an annex.

301.   Provide data, analysis and comments on the service coverage
(numbers of people served) according to service standards (type of
facility and quality of service) for each delineated area, selecting
applicable categories from the following list:

— Estimate the number of people served by:

o unimproved systems:
   - shallow wells, rivers, lakes and, natural and
   man-made ponds,

o improved point sources:
   - wells with handpumps, rainwater storage tanks, etc.,

o piped water systems (individual connections and
   standpipes);

-- For those people served by piped water systems, estimate:

    o   villages and people served by shared systems (consumer source and transmission facilities),

    o   house connections (supplying indoor taps),

    o   courtyard taps,

    o   public standpipes;

-- For handpumps and standpipes, provide general information to explain the convenience to consumers such as:

    o   waiting times,

    o   distance from homes,

    o   availabilities within all ethnic areas,

    o   existence of standpipes on both sides of roads,

    o   types of containers used to carry water to homes,

    o   use of standpipes by water vendors;

-- Note which sources are used for drinking, bathing, animals, etc;

-- Describe those groups not being served by any improved water supply system (including those supplied by vendors, etc.) and explain why they do not receive any service;

-- Describe how water is obtained, by whom, how much, etc. Children, women, men? Explain the preferred sources and use patterns of each group. Describe users' attitudes toward quality: preferences and constraints. Include anecdotal material which helps explain the use or non-use of certain sources;

-- Provide available water quality data (bacteriological and chemical analyses) for various sources of water;

-- Include information on shortages and seasonal variations in supply and estimate the amount of water that would be used if shortages did not exist;

-- Analyze the frequency of breakdowns, including the time taken to restore service;

-- Explain how (and how much as a percentage of total cost) the user contributes towards:

o construction,

o operation and maintenance;

-- Describe user charges levied by village or water agency and payment to vendors and concessionaires;

-- Provide a comprehensive critique of the various water supply facilities, with particular comments on their weaknesses or problems and on possible means to overcome such problems. Refer to positive experiences with system facilities in the program or nearby area for guidance as to possible remedies to identified problems;

Existing Sanitation Services and Population Served

302.   As in the case of water supply facilities, this section should summarize and assess all existing sanitation and waste disposal facilities in the program area and estimate the number of people served by each. All methods used to dispose of human wastes and wastewater by people in the area should be described, including on-site sanitation systems and sewers.

-- discuss with selected local informants (such as teachers or health workers) alternative technologies in light of socio-cultural, economic and technical constraints;

-- pay particular attention to each method of waste disposal. Constraints on increasing services should be highlighted.

NOTE: Use maps to delineate areas where the different disposal methods are used and schematic diagrams, charts and tables of data to summarize information. Additional background material can be presented in an annex.

303.   Provide for each sanitation system:

-- typical sketches of independent sanitation systems (latrines, septic tanks, etc);

-- estimates of the number of each type of sanitation systems and comments on their design, construction, operation and effectiveness;

-- information on informal reuse patterns of excreta, if any (for pigs, fish, fertilizer, etc.);

-- information on the role of the private sector in providing services (such as septic tank emptying and nightsoil collection);

-- a description of existing wastewater treatment processes, if any (including objectives, design criteria and operational effectiveness);

304.   Provide data, analysis and comments on the service coverage (numbers of people served) according to service standards (type of facility and quality of service) for each sanitation system, using appropriate topics from the following list:

-- Provide a breakdown of the total population in the project area by groups according to the way in which they dispose of their body wastes:

o primitive (defecation on the ground),

o individual on-site sanitation facilities (latrines, septic tanks, etc.),

o communal sanitation facilities,

o sewerage;

-- Review any social, cultural or religious considerations which may affect sanitation practices;

-- Describe any sanitation facilities which may have been provided and are not in use, and explain why. Describe the actual disposal practices in such cases;

-- Discuss excreta disposal practices of children and note use of facilities in public buildings, especially schools;

-- Explain how sullage (greywater) from households is disposed of;

-- Assess the effectiveness of the various sanitation systems in the area in terms of:

o costs,

  o effect on domestic hygiene and public health generally,

  o protection of water quality;

 — Provide a comprehensive critique of the various sanitation systems and their use, with special emphasis on existing problems and on possible means to overcome such problems. Refer to positive experiences with sanitation facilities within the program or adjacent areas for guidance as to possible remedies to identified problems.

Need for the Program

305. This key section draws conclusions about the need for a program in light of population patterns and projections, existing service coverage and standards, and prospects for improving and expanding existing systems. If the critical analysis of existing water supply and sanitation systems has indicated that major improvements in service can be obtained by remedying weaknesses in present systems, the first priority should be to make the necessary corrections and appropriate recommendations should be included in the project description.

306. This final section of the chapter basically summarizes why the existing systems cannot cope with present and projected demands for services and forms the basis of the program which is to be defined in the next chapter. Topics to be considered here include:

 -- a description of the consequences these deficiencies in water and sanitation services will have on the present and future population in the area if major improvements are not made;

 -- an outline of priorities to:

  o improve and expand water supply and sanitation services,

  o meet basic human needs as well as demands by industry and commerce in the program area;

 -- an assessment of the need for hygiene education and the promotion of the use of water and sanitation services to improve public health in the project area;

 -- comments on the urgency of project implementation.

IV.   THE PROPOSED PROGRAM

307.   This chapter should provide the basic details about the
proposed program. A brief description should be presented, including
the objectives, the number of people to receive the services, the cost
of the program, the time to carry out the works, the sub-project
selection criteria, the types of systems and facilities, the sources of
water, the community involvement, and participating agencies and their
responsibilities.

Objectives

308.   Program objectives should be expressed in two ways. General
development objectives should include estimates of:

-- health improvements;

-- reduced burden in carrying water and expected impact,
   particularly on women and children (savings in time and
   energy);

-- improved living standards and productivity of users;

-- institutional improvements and staff development.

Another possible general objective for the project is to be used as a
model for replication by similar programs elsewhere in the country.

309.   Operational objectives concern improvements in service
coverage and standards for water supply and sanitation. Each objective
should be quantified (to the extent practicable), and a schedule for
achieving these objectives presented.

NOTE: Future evaluation of the program will measure its results
         in terms of this original statement of objectives. This
         provides further rationale for developing realistic
         objectives.

Sub-Project Users and Their Perspectives

310.   Define by number and location the people (and, if appropriate,
the institutions) who will benefit from the project. This estimate of
sub-project beneficiaries should be realistic, taking into account
probable constraints on the acceptance and use of services.

311.   Indicate whether any people in the area will not benefit from the program and explain why they will not have access to improved services after the program is implemented.

NOTE: Longer term solutions for serving these people should also be given.

312.   Explain the selection, role, involvement and input of potential users of sub-projects in the planning process. Explain what plans exist to involve users in helping to construct sub-projects and eventually operating them.

NOTE: The role of women as active participants in program and sub-project planning, implementation and operation should be explicitly considered as they are frequently "managers" of water and sanitation services at the household level. Women should be involved in gathering and analyzing data about project users.

Rehabilitation of Existing Facilities

313.   Explain any proposals to rehabilitate and improve existing sector facilities. Explain why existing facilities need to be rehabilitated and discuss what plans have been formulated to ensure that the proposed project systems will not themselves fall into disuse.

Program Description

314.   Define the program and outline its components, with maps, photos and drawings as appropriate. Describe necessary support activities, such as health education, training of local operators, etc. Indicate how sub-projects are selected for inclusion in the program and how user communities participate in this selection process and the choice of selection criteria. Describe sub-project design standards. Summarize information for presentation in the report and provide more detailed information, if necessary, in annexes.

NOTE: Water supply and sanitation components of the program should be described separately with the emphasis depending on whether or not both services are covered.

313.   For sub-projects and their water supply and sanitation facilities, describe:

    -- the sub-project selection criteria and the process by which they were determined;

-- how the sub-project implementation priority was established;

-- the location, capacity and components of sub-projects to be implemented during the first year of the program;

-- the status and degree of preparation of sub-projects to be implemented in subsequent years of the program;

-- design criteria for water supply and sanitation facilities;

-- the standard designs available or under preparation (technical specifications, dimensions, materials, etc. and method of construction);

-- systems with shared facilities (source, transmission) to reduce costs; and

-- the location and capacity of water resources for sub-projects and activities to obtain this information if not available;

-- whether and how components to be located in houses and yards, such as water and wastewater service pipes, plumbing and on-site waste disposal facilities are included. If these essential components are not included, then estimate their cost and explain how they will be financed and built;

-- consulting services required, if any, to attain the objectives of the project.

316. For the support activities, rationalize and describe:

-- components to strengthen the performance of sector agencies (such as staff training, adequate transportation, spare parts and storage). Specify the numbers of people involved, achievement targets, the timing of programs, responsibilities for their completion, and so on;

-- components for other project participants e.g. training of contractors, extension workers and project users. Again, specify precisely what is to be done, when, by which agencies, the personnel required, how the community is to be involved, and how this is to be coordinated with construction.

NOTE: These components are described in more detail in paragraphs 318-325.

Cost Estimates

317.   Provide a summary of the estimated cost of the entire program and for each sub-project for the first year of the program implementation.

   -- Make realistic provision for unexpected costs (physical contingencies) for each component;

   NOTE: Items with greater uncertainty (for example, wells to be located where the geology is not fully known) should have greater contingencies.

   -- Estimate base prices for each element (at a specified time) for each year of implementation before applying an allowance for price increases (inflation) in the future;

   -- Provide a summary of expected annual costs;

   -- Break down costs into foreign exchange (if importation of goods is necessary) and local currency components and explain the basis of the breakdown;

   -- Explain fully how the costs were estimated and list all basic assumptions, particularly those for unit prices, physical contingencies and price increases;

   -- Compare the cost estimates for the proposed sub-projects with those for recent similar or related projects in the region or country.

Implementation Responsibilities

318.   Generally speaking, the fewer institutions involved, the fewer the implementation problems. In some programs, different institutions will be responsible for different parts of the program and delays in participation could cause problems. Paying attention to coordination can avoid this. In one case, for example, one agency was responsible for drilling the wells with its own staff and by contract; another for organizing the communities; one for rural water supply planning; one for constructing the systems; the village associations for administering and operating the systems; and yet another for health education and sanitation. Because the functions were clearly defined, the program was implemented satisfactorily.

   -- Identify all institutions and voluntary organizations involved;

-- Describe their specific functions/responsibilities;

-- Describe the mechanism for coordination;

-- Comment on the compatibility of these institutions to carry out their tasks and identify necessary assistance (staff training, funding, etc.) to be carried out;

-- Designate the lead agency to manage implementation of the program and outline proposed arrangements to coordinate all inputs;

-- List materials, if any, to be imported and explain necessary procedures to acquire them.

319.   It should not be assumed that every village is interested in having water supply and sanitation facilities. Prior to initiating the work, it is essential to involve each village in the decision on how to provide the facilities, and arrange for their operation and maintenance. If people are not sufficiently motivated, they generally will not use the facilities properly nor take care of them.

-- Indicate how community was consulted and motivated;

-- Describe how participation will be organized, what technical assistance will be provided, how it will be funded;

-- Identify all groups (government, non-government, and local community organizations) whose input is necessary for successful project implementation at the local level and provide a clear statement of all tasks for which each group is responsible;

-- Present proposals for monitoring and evaluating sub-project effectiveness against original objectives, including monitoring criteria and the type of reports expected to be submitted.

NOTE: Voluntary organizations have achieved excellent results through community participation and user training. Their potential role should be considered and described.

Implementation Schedule

320.   Provide a detailed and realistic implementation schedule for all project components including community consultation, staff training, promotion and health education, complete with a graphical summary.

Depict the tasks of each group involved, with activities illustrated logically according to implementation plans.

321.   Indicate whether consultants (local or external) are required to assist the implementing agency and how they will be selected.

322.   For physical components, show all activities, including:

-- the preparation of bidding documents, bidding review, award of contracts, mobilization, construction and commissioning;

-- describe organization of self-help work;

-- indicate what parts of the system will be built by contractor, by force account, by self-help labor.

NOTE: Where self-help activities are planned, allow for seasonal variations in the availability of local labor, and the time required for community consultation and mobilization.

323.   Describe:

-- Who will mobilize and control execution of work by village labor;

-- The program for purchasing materials and equipment;

-- Availability of local supplies, materials and labor;

-- What skilled labor is needed and how will it be provided;

-- If the villagers are to provide unskilled labor, do they need basic tools and who will provide them.

324.   Ascertain critical steps logically and list them separately. Include administrative steps such as the provision of the required budget, land acquisition and approval for water abstraction.

325.   The proposed program for which financial assistance is being sought may not include some components of a comprehensive development program. For example, health and nutrition programs may, for administrative reasons, not be included in the defined program. Clearly describe such complementary inputs and how these efforts are organized, linked and funded.

Operation and Maintenance

326.   Describe all groups (government and non-government) which will be involved in operation and maintenance after the facilities are built.

-- Describe, in particular, how any "self-help" community operation and maintenance is to be organized, what technical assistance will be provided, by whom and under what conditions. Consider also the role of women in operation and maintenance, both community wide and at the household level;

-- Estimate annual costs for future operation and maintenance.

Environmental Impacts

327.   Briefly describe the various environmental impacts which are expected to result, including those on public health and/or water, air and land resources. For each impact discuss proposals to reduce adverse impacts and increase positive impacts through project design and operation. Distinguish between temporary or short-term impacts associated with project construction and longer-term impacts of project operation.

328.   Provide a general prognosis of changes:

-- Where data permit, include a list of diseases related to water supply and sanitation, including present morbidity and mortality rates and outline the improvements expected to occur after the sub-project become operational;

-- Explain qualitatively the probable consequences of expected improvements in health. Indicate time and energy savings for women and children. Note any improvements in nutrition from use of extra water or reclaimed wastewater in domestic agriculture, i.e. vegetables, fruits, poultry and pigs;

-- Outline possible negative impacts, such as the risk of introducing schistosomiasis, or spreading malaria by creating reservoirs or increasing stagnant water in residential areas if drainage and sewerage improvements do not keep up with increases in the supply of water.

329.   Examine possible impacts on water resources for the water supply component.

-- Analyze the effect of withdrawing water from surface or groundwater sources;

-- Estimate the reliability of the water source, particularly in drought conditions, bearing in mind probable future developments and especially major water uses such as irrigation;

-- Examine the prospects for future changes in the quality of water at the source.

330.   Similarly examine possible water resources impacts for the sanitation component.

-- Estimate the impact on local surface water resources of disposal systems which discharge to the nearest water course such as a stream, river or lake;

-- Consider impacts on local groundwater of on-site sanitation systems;

-- Evaluate existing drainage arrangements when these have to handle increased quantities of sullage water and consider all appropriate reuse possibilities;

IV. INSTITUTIONAL AND FINANCIAL ASPECTS

331.   In the long term, project benefits depend at least as much on the organization(s) responsible for operating and maintaining the project as they do on the organization which constructs it. Sometimes the same organization is involved in both stages. Where separate entities are involved (particularly village organizations) in construction and in operation and maintenance, detailed arrangements for a smooth transition from the construction stage to the operational stage are necessary.

332.   Financial resources for operation and maintenance must be available at the local and regional (government) level, otherwise a lack of funds will result in lack of maintenance and eventual breakdown of facilities. This chapter describes institutional and financial arrangements necessary to ensure permanent satisfactory performance of the facilities constructed as part of the water supply and sanitation program.

Organization and Management

333.   Describe operational and management aspects of existing and proposed organizations which will assist communities to build and later operate and maintain the existing and expanded water supply and sanitation facilities. Topics to be discussed include:

-- legal basis and possible legal constraints;

-- organization charts, existing or proposed;

-- the extent and location of facilities to be operated by the organizations and by communities and the relationship and working arrangements with user communities;

-- the relationship between different functional groups (planning, design, construction, operations, finance, etc.) and between different regional offices;

-- relationships with other government agencies and organizations involved in sector activities (engineering, public health, volunteer, environment, procurement, etc.);

-- the process for developing policies and making major decisions.

334.   Pay particular attention to those organizations responsible for program support activities or software (particularly hygiene education) which are expected to proceed along with the operation of physical facilities for water supply and sanitation. The role of these organizations and of possible related groups (social workers, local cooperatives, women's groups, extension workers, etc.) should be carefully examined. Explain

-- arrangements made for effective communications (particularly for emergency maintenance assistance) and record keeping;

-- arrangements for the purchasing and storekeeping of materials and equipment and its supply to communities at their request.

Staffing and Training

335.   The effectiveness of an organization depends primarily on its employees. This section should assess the present situation in terms of management and personnel.

-- Explain the policies and practices of the lead agency in using either the private sector or other public sector organizations to provide personnel assistance (consultants or contractors);

-- Comment on the capability of the agency to attract and retain new staff and discuss the conditions of employment, career prospects and job satisfaction as perceived by staff at various levels;

-- Comment on capability and staffing of other agencies to the extent they affect the program.

336.   <u>Future staffing and training plans</u> merit special attention.

-- Compare future staff requirements to the existing situation and define the potential shortfall (if any).

-- Outline agency plans to recruit required staff in the future and to provide appropriate staff motivation, training and retraining.

-- Discuss the possible need to retrain and employ people who may lose their jobs because of the project (water vendors, night soil collectors, etc.)

Financial History

337.   Describe the existing financial situation of the organizations (lead agency, villages) which will operate and maintain sub-project facilities and provide technical assistance.

-- Discuss the overall financial position of the organizations (past and present) and explain the major expenditures and sources of operating income.

-- Discuss any financial problems, including their impact on operations and performance and therefore on services to be provided under this program.

Charges for Services

338.   Funds will have to be provided on an annual basis to pay for the staff and materials that may be needed to periodically inspect and make repairs to the facilities that the villagers cannot make. Some of these funds may have to come from the government budget and the sub-project designs should take this into account. Supporting staff should also advise local operators and villagers on the proper

operation, administration and maintenance of the system. The funds to be provided will depend on the area covered, the number of supervisory personnel employed, the types of systems involved, the level of competence of the villagers, and salary scales.

339.   It should be verified that the community wants to have a water system and is willing and able to participate, at least by paying proposed charges to cover operating costs. This is particularly true in the case of public wells and standpipes. In some villages there is a well-defined social structure and organization that can be utilized to collect such charges; in others, a new organization may need to be established. Experience in many countries has shown that if an organization representing the community has signed a formal written agreement, good results can be achieved. Such agreements should be signed before construction is started. Describe:

-- Arrangements at village level to recover funds for operation and maintenance.

-- Proposed rates and the percentage of income they represent.

-- Provisions at government level (national, state, district) to financially support communities for tasks not covered by village contribution (such as central planning, spare parts, housing, etc.).

-- Outline any established or proposed policies for past and future revenues.

Future Financial Situation

340.   Continued operation and maintenance, without which even the best projects will fail, depends on adequate finances. Every attempt should be made to ensure adequate generation of funds from users for at least the local operation and maintenance costs. It is generally better to encourage grants for project implementation rather than for operations, given the uncertainty about the permanence of grant funding. Provide financial forecasts for both the agency providing technical assistance and support and the sub-project operators:

-- State explicitly all basic assumptions for the financial forecasts, including the assumed terms and conditions of all financial sources.

-- Demonstrate the future financial health of the project agency and village organizations, particularly their ability to cover all operating and maintenance expenditures.

Financing Plan

341.   This section summarizes all sources of funds needed for the implementation of the program.

- — Identify possible sources and terms of finance (internal and external) to meet the total cost of the program and prepare year-by-year estimates of cash flows for the sub-project implementation. Indicate what funds will be contributed by:

    o the user community,

    o governments (local, provincial, national),

    o development   assistance   agencies   (multilateral, bilateral, non-governmental);

- —— Explain carefully the procedures that are involved and the sequence followed to obtain the funds required for implementation of the project.

342.   International financial agencies do not participate in programs or projects where accountability is in doubt. They normally require, at a minimum, that an accounting and reporting system, capable of reporting all project transactions accurately and promptly, will be operational from the start of project implementation. Hence this section needs to discuss appropriate arrangements for future accounting and reporting.

V.   CONCLUSIONS AND RECOMMENDATIONS

343.   This chapter states whether the proposed program is feasible when judged from all perspectives and recommends actions to be taken for its implementation. It also discusses issues and risks associated with project implementation.

Justification

344.   Discuss in qualitative terms why the proposed program is justified and should proceed.

- —— Summarize how the program will satisfy the objectives and confirm that the it is the most cost-effective solution to meeting these objectives;

-- Explain the interest of the intended users and their role (past and proposed) in sub-project preparation and implementation. Make specific reference to the willingness and capability of the intended beneficiaries to support sub-projects, including the payment of charges for services;

-- Discuss the effects of not proceeding with the project.

Conclusions

345.   Summarize briefly the conclusions which demonstrate that the program is feasible:

-- technically;

-- financially;

-- socially and culturally;

-- institutionally.

Issues and Risks

346.   Identify all issues which may pose a risk to program implementation and operation (such as funding shortfalls, political instability, etc.). Make a judgment as to the gravity of each risk and suggest ways of minimizing such risks.

347.   Examine the consequences of small and large changes in the major assumptions on which the report is based, such as:

-- ineffective organization and management of many discrete program activities;

-- lack of cooperation between participating organizations;

-- delays in implementation of training and support activities;

-- insufficient community participation;

-- delays in sub-project implementation;

-- increases in cost.

Recommended Actions

348.   List the key actions which need to be taken in order to approve, implement and operate sub-projects successfully. Include any policy questions which need to be resolved.

-- Each recommendation should name the agency or individual to be responsible for the action, with a suggested timetable;

-- Provide an outline scope of work where detailed activities need to be undertaken (such as water resource investigations).

NOTE: Emphasize potential difficulties which could critically delay progress.

349.   Indicate specific actions which the agency responsible for program implementation can commence so as to avoid delays while necessary agreements are reached on program and sub-project approval and financing.

F. BIBLIOGRAPHY

Note: This Bibliography is based on the POETRI Standard Basic Library
of the International Reference Centre for Community Water Supply
and Sanitaton.

I. GENERAL

Cairncross, Sandy and Feachem, Richard G.
ENVIRONMENTAL HEALTH ENGINEERING IN THE TROPICS
John Wiley & Sons Ltd., Chichester and New York, 1983

Dangerfield, Bernard J. (ed)
WATER SUPPLY AND SANITATION IN DEVELOPING COUNTRIES
Institution of Water Engineers and Scientists, London, 1983

Feachem, R.G. et al
SANITATION AND DISEASE - Health Aspects of Excreta and Wastewater
   Management
The Johns Hopkins University Press, Baltimore, 1981

Feachem, R.G. et al
WATER, HEALTH AND ENVIRONMENT - An Interdisciplinary Evaluation
Tri-Med Books Ltd., London, 1978

Feachem, R.G. et al
WATER, WASTES AND HEALTH IN HOT CLIMATES
John Wiley & Sons Ltd., Chichester and New York, 1977

Pacey, A. (ed)
WATER FOR THE THOUSAND MILLION
Pergamon Press, Oxford, 1979

Pacey, A. (ed)
SANITATION IN DEVELOPING COUNTRIES
Oxfam/Ross Institute, Oxford, 5-9 July 1977
John Wiley & Sons, London, 1978

Saunders, R.J., Warford, J.J.
VILLAGE WATER SUPPLY - Economics and Policy in the Developing World
World Bank Research Publications
Johns Hopkins University Press, Baltimore, 1976

Schiller, E.J., Droste, R.L. (ed)
WATER SUPPLY AND SANITATION IN DEVELOPING COUNTRIES
Ann Arbor Science Publishers, Ann Arbor, 1982

Tinker, J. (ed)
WATER AND SANITATION FOR ALL
Press Briefing Document No. 22
Earthscan, London, 1980

White, A.U., Seviour, C.
RURAL WATER SUPPLY AND SANITATION IN LESS DEVELOPED COUNTRIES
International Development Research Centre, Ottawa, 1974

WATER SUPPLY AND WASTE DISPOSAL
World Bank, September, 1980

DRINKING WATER AND SANITATION, 1981-1990: A Way to Health
World Health Organization, Geneva

THE INTERNATIONAL DRINKING WATER SUPPLY AND SANITATION DECADE
  DIRECTORY DONOR CATALOGUE
World Health Organization, Geneva, 1981

II. PLANNING, MANAGEMENT, EVALUATION AND TRAINING

Cairncross, S., Carruthers, I., Curtis, D., et al
EVALUATION FOR VILLAGE WATER SUPPLY PLANNING
International Reference Centre for Community Water Supply and
    Sanitation, the Hague, 1979, (Technical Paper Series no. 15)

Donaldson, D.
PLANNING WATER AND SANITATION SYSTEMS FOR SMALL COMMUNITIES
In: International Training Seminar on Community Water Supply in
    Developing Countries, (Amsterdam, 1976)
International Reference Centre for Community Water Supply and
    Sanitation, the Hague, 1977, (Bulletin no. 10)

GUIDELINES ON HEALTH ASPECTS OF PLUMBING
A publication jointly with the World Health Organization
International Reference Centre for Community Water Supply and
    Sanitation, the Hague, 1982

Kalbermatten, J.M., Julius, D.S., Gunnerson, C.G.
APPROPRIATE TECHNOLOGY FOR WATER SUPPLY AND SANITATION
A Planner's Guide
World Bank, December, 1980

Kalbermatten, J.M., Julius, D.S., Gunnerson, C.G.
APPROPRIATE TECHNOLOGY FOR WATER SUPPLY AND SANITATION
A Summary of Technical and Economic Options
Johns Hopkins University Press, 1980

Lamson-Scribner, F.H., Huang, J.W.
MUNICIPAL WATER SUPPLY CASE STUDIES
Economic Development Institute, World Bank, 1978

Pacey, A. (ed)
RURAL SANITATION: PLANNING AND APPRAISAL
An Oxfam Document
Intermediate Technology Publications Ltd., London, 1980

REPUBLIC OF TERRANIA
A Case Study
WHO/World Bank Cooperative Programme
World Health Organization, Geneva, 1980

III. TECHNOLOGY

A. WATER SUPPLY

Beyer, M.G.
DRINKING WATER FOR EVERY VILLAGE
Choosing Appropriate Technologies
Assignment Children, 1976, no. 34 (April-June)

Cairncross, S., Feachem, R.G.
SMALL WATER SUPPLIES
Ross Institute, London, 1978
(Bulletin no. 10)

Huisman, L., Azevedo Netto, J.M., de, Sundaresaon, B.B.,
  Lanoix, J.N., Hofkes, E.H. (ed)
SMALL COMMUNITY WATER SUPPLIES
International Reference Centre for Community Water Supply and
  Sanitation, the Hague, August, 1981

McJunkin, F.E.
WATER, ENGINEERS, DEVELOPMENT AND DISEASE IN THE TROPICS
U.S. Agency for International Development, Washington, D.C., 1975

PRACTICAL SOLUTIONS IN DRINKING WATER SUPPLY AND WASTES DISPOSAL
  FOR DEVELOPING COUNTRIES
International Reference Centre for Community Water Supply and
  Sanitation, the Hague, 1982 (Revised edition)

Rajagopalan, S., Shiffman, M.A.
GUIDE ON SIMPLE SANITARY MEASURES FOR THE CONTROL OF ENTERIC
  DISEASES
World Health Organization, Geneva, 1974 (Booklet, 103)

RURAL WATER SUPPLY IN DEVELOPING COUNTRIES
Proceedings of a workshop of training held in Zomba, Malawi
  5-12 August, 1980
International Development Research Centre, Ottawa, 1980

SIMPLIFIED PROCEDURES FOR WATER EXAMINATION - A LABORATORY MANUAL
American Water Works Association, New York, 1975
(supplement published in 1977)

SURVEILLANCE OF DRINKING WATER QUALITY
World Health Organizaion, Geneva, 1976
(WHO Monograph Series, no 63)

GUIDELINES FOR DRINKING WATER QUALITY
World Health Organization, Geneva, 1982

B. Sanitation

Feachem, R.G., Cairncross, S.
SMALL EXCRETA-DISPOSAL SYSTEMS
Ross Institute London, 1978
(Bulletin no. 8)

Kalbermatten, J.M., Julius, D.S., Gunnerson, C.G., Mara, D.
APPROPRIATE SANITATION ALTERNATIVES
A Sanitation Field Manual
World Bank, December, 1980

Mara, D.
SEWAGE TREATMENT IN HOT CLIMATE
John Wiley & Sons, London, 1978.

Morgan, Peter R., Mara, D. Duncan
VENTILATED IMPROVED PIT LATRINES: RECENT DEVELOPMENT IN ZIMBABWE
World Bank, 1982

Nielsen, J.H., Clauson-Kaas, M.
APPROPRIATE SANITATION
COWI-consult Consulting Engineers and Planners AS
Virum, Denmark, 1980

Rybzynski, W., et al
LOW-COST TECHNOLOGY OPTIONS FOR SANITATION
International Development Research Centre, Ottawa, 1978

SANITATION IN DEVELOPING COUNTRIES
Proceedings of a workshop on Training held in Lobatse, Botswana
    14-20 August, 1980
International Development Research Centre, Ottawa, 1981

Simmons, J.D., Newman, J.O., Rose, C.W., Rose, E.E.
SMALL DIAMETER VARIABLE GRADE GRAVITY SEWERS FOR SEPTIC TANK
    EFFLUENT
Proceedings of the American Society of Agricultural Engineers,
    Third National Symposium on Individual and Small Community Sewage
    Treatment, December 14-15, 1981

Wagner, E.G., Lanoix, J.N.
EXCRETA DISPOSAL FUR RURAL AND SMALL COMMUNITIES
World Health Organization, Geneva, 1958 (reprinted 1971)
Monography Series, no. 39

C. MONOGRAPHS

Cox, C.R.
OPERATION AND CONTROL OF WATER TREATMENT PROCESSES
World Health Organization, 1974
(Monograph Series, no. 49)

Dijk, J.V. van, Oomen, J.H.C.M.
SLOW SAND FILTRATION FOR COMMUNITY WATER SUPPLY IN DEVELOPING
    COUNTRIES - A DESIGN AND CONSTRUCTION MANUAL
International Reference Centre for Community Water Supply and
    Sanitation, the Hague, 1978 (Technical Paper no. 11)

Gibson, U., Singer, R.
SMALL WELLS MANUAL
Premier Press, U.S.A., 1969

Hofkes, E.H.
RAINWATER HARVESTING FOR DRINKING WATER SUPPLY
International Reference Centre for Community Water Supply and
    Sanitation, the Hague, 1981
IRC Study Paper
(Partly published in 'World Water', October, 1981)

McJunkin, F.E.
HANDPUMPS FOR USE IN DRINKING WATER SUPPLIES IN DEVELOPING
    COUNTRIES
International Reference Centre for Community Water Supply and
    Sanitation, the Hague, 1977 (Technical Paper no. 13)

SHALLOW WELLS
DHV Consulting Engineers, Amersfoort, the Netherlands, 1978

TYPICAL DESIGNS FOR ENGINEERS COMPONENTS IN RURAL WATER SUPPLY
WHO Regional Office for South-East Asia, New Delhi,
(WHO Regional Publications, South East Asia Series no. 2)

Watt, S., Wood, W.E.
HAND DUG WELLS AND THEIR CONSTRUCTION
Intermediate Technology Publications Ltd., London, 1976

IV. COMMUNICATIONS SUPPORT, COMMUNITY PARTICIPATION AND HEALTH
     EDUCATION

     Elmendorf, M., Buckles, P.
     SOCIOCULTURAL ASPECTS OF WATER SUPPLY AND EXCRETA DISPOSAL
     World Bank, December, 1980

     Glennie, C.
     A MODEL FOR THE DEVELOPMENT OF A SELF-HELP WATER SUPPLY PROGRAM
     World Bank, 1982

     Martin, Patricia A., et al
     COMMUNITY PARTICIPATION IN PRIMARY HEALTH CARE
     Primary Health Care Issues, Series 1, Number 5
     American Public Health ASsociation, Washington DC, 1983

     Perret, H., Lethem, F.
     HUMAN FACTORS IN PROJECT WORK
     World Bank, 1980

     Perret, H.
     PLANNING OF COMMUNICATION SUPPORT (INFORMATION, MOTIVATION AND
       EDUCATION) IN SANITATION PROJECTS AND PROGRAMS
     World Bank, 1983

     Perret, H.
     SOCIAL FEASIBILITY ANALYSIS IN LOW-COST SANITATION PROJECTS
     World Bank, 1983

     Perret, H.
     USING COMMUNICATION SUPPORT IN PROJECTS
     World Bank, 1983

     Simpson-Hébert, Mayling
     METHODS FOR GATHERING SOCIO-CULTURAL DATA FOR WATER SUPPLY AND
       SANITATION PROJECTS
     World Bank, 1983

     White, Alastair
     COMMUNITY PARTICIPATION IN WATER AND SANITATION
     Concepts, Strategies and Methods
     International Reference Centre for Community Water Supply and
       Sanitation, the Hague, 1981
     (Technical Paper no. 17)

     Whyte, Ann
     TOWARDS A USER-CHOICE PHILOSOPHY IN RURAL WATER SUPPLY PROGRAMMES
     Assignment Children 1976, no. 34 (April-June)
     UNICEF, Geneva

Wijk-Sijbesma, C. van
PARTICIPATION AND EDUCATION IN COMMUNITY WATER SUPPLY AND
    SANITATION PROGRAMMES
A selected and annotated bibliography
International Reference Centre for Community Water Supply and
    Sanitation, The Hague, 1980
(Bulletin Series no. 13)

SUGGESTED GUIDELINES FOR INCORPORATING COMMUNITY COMMUNICATIONS AND
    PARTICIPATION IN PROJECT FORMULATION
UNDP, Division of Information

SOURCES OF FURTHER INFORMATION

1. Water and Wastes Adviser
    Transportation and Water Department
    The World Bank
    Washington, DC 20433
    U.S.A.

Useful material is being generated under four UNDP Special Projects undertaken by the World Bank in support of the International Drinking Water Supply and Sanitation Decade:

(1) Information and Training Program in Low-Cost Water Supply and Sanitation.

(2) Development and Implementation of Low-Cost Sanitation Investment Projects.

(3) Field Testing and Technological Development of Rural Water Supply Handpumps.

(4) Research and Development in Integrated Resource Recovery.

Various results of these research projects are available, including computer programs for designing water distribution systems, developing cost and water demand functions, analyzing the financial feasibility of water projects, and designing sanitary sewers. Material produced by these projects, which is constantly being improved, can be obtained from the World Bank.

2. International Reference Centre for Community Water Supply and
        Sanitation
    P.O. Box 5500
    2280 HM Rijswijk
    The Netherlands

    Documents and reference material.

3. Environmental Sanitation Information Center
    Asian Institute of Technology
    Box 2754
    Bangkok
    Thailand

    Documents and reference material

THE
PROJECT CYCLE

BY

WARREN C. BAUM

THE PROJECT CYCLE

If the question, "What does the World Bank do?" had to be answered in a few words, those words would be: "It lends for development projects." The Bank's main business is to lend for specific projects, carefully selected and prepared, thoroughly appraised, closely supervised, and systematically evaluated. Since opening its doors in 1946, the Bank—in the context of this pamphlet, the International Bank for Reconstruction and Development and its soft-loan affiliate, the International Development Association (IDA), which began operations in 1961—has made some 3,094 development loans and credits for a total of more than $92 billion. Of these, the overwhelming majority, over 90 percent, have been for specific projects such as schools, crop production programs, hydroelectric power dams, roads, and fertilizer plants.

This concentration on project lending is directed at ensuring that Bank funds are invested in sound, productive projects that contribute to the development of a borrowing country's economy as well as to its capacity to repay the loan. The Bank is both a developmental and a financial institution, and each project for which it lends must satisfy both features of the institution.

The numbers of projects and the amounts loaned have grown markedly over recent years. In the early 1950s, the Bank was making fewer than twenty loans a year, mostly in Europe and Latin America, totaling about $400 million. In fiscal year 1967, there were sixty-seven loans, more widely spread geographically, totaling $1.1 billion. In the fiscal year ending in June 1981, 246 loans, totaling $12.3 billion, were approved for ninety countries.

There has been no less a change in the character of projects. Bank lending has become increasingly development oriented in terms of borrowing countries, development strategy, sectors of lending, and project design.

— In terms of *countries:* Lending has been directed increasingly toward the poor and less developed countries in Asia, Africa, and Latin America.

— In terms of *development strategy:* The so-called trickle-down theory, which assumes that the benefits of growth will eventually reach the masses of the poor, has been replaced in the Bank by a more balanced approach, combining accelerated growth with a direct attack on poverty through programs to raise the productivity and living standards of the rural and urban poor.

— In terms of *sectors:* The emphasis has shifted from basic infrastructure (roads, railways, power) and industry to more comprehensive programs aimed at growth, provision of basic services, and improvment of income distribution. While infrastructure continues to be important, lending for agriculture and rural development, oil and gas, urban sites and services, water supply and sanitation, small-scale enterprises, education, health, population, and nutrition has been introduced or greatly expanded.

— In terms of *project design:* Greater attention is given in all sectors, both new and traditional, to income distribution and employment, development of local resources and institutions, training of local personnel, impact on environment, and overcoming social and cultural constraints. The Bank has not diminished, however, the attention that it has always paid to market forces, realistic pricing, good management, and the recovery, where feasible, of project costs to permit adequate maintenance and replication.

This evolution in the development orientation—and in the quality—of Bank lending can be illustrated, at the risk of oversimplification, by comparing a "typical" loan of the 1950s with a "typical" loan of the 1970s.

The 1950s loan might be for power generation in a middle-income developing country. In a sense it would be an "enclave" project, designed and supervised by foreign consultants, executed by foreign contractors and suppliers, and managed with the help of expatriates. The technical and financial viability of the project would be analyzed, as would its organization and management, but little attention would be paid to its setting within the energy sector, to how the electricity would be distributed, and to the impact of the level and structure of tariffs on power consumption.

The loan of the 1970s would be for rural development in a low-income developing country. It would provide an integrated package of goods and services (extension, credit, marketing, storage, infrastructure, research) to raise the productivity and living standards of farmers. Existing local institutions would be strengthened or new ones established;

local staff would be used as much as possible, with the help of extensive training programs; low-cost design and appropriate technology would be emphasized, giving greater opportunities for local contractors and sources of supply; a system of monitoring and evaluation would be built in to help adjust the project as it went forward and to draw lessons for future projects; and attention would be paid to cost recovery from beneficiaries so that the project would be replicable.

Notwithstanding this record of growth and change, the Bank is still dealing with a relatively small number of quite large projects; the average loan is now about $50 million for a total project investment of $140 million. Bank-assisted projects can have an important demonstration effect and can encourage other investors to supplement Bank lending with their own, as cofinancers or separately; approximately one-third of Bank assisted projects in 1981 had cofinancing from foreign sources.

Every Bank-assisted project must contribute substantially to development objectives and be economically, technically, and financially sound. No two projects are alike; each has its own history, and lending has to be tailored to its circumstances. On the other hand, each project passes through a cycle that, with some variations, is common to all. This pamphlet will discuss the phases of the project cycle—identification, preparation, appraisal, negotiation and presentation to the Executive Directors, implementation and supervision, and evaluation—and the Bank's role in each of them. Each phase leads to the next, and the last phases, in turn, produce new project approaches and ideas and lead to the identification of new projects, making the cycle self-renewing.

The Bank's role in the project cycle is performed largely by its projects staff, who now number about 1,300 drawn from 100 nationalities. Projects staff comprise almost three-quarters of all operational staff employed by the Bank and nearly half of all professional staff. Though there are substantial groups of economists, financial analysts, and various kinds of engineers, an extraordinary variety of other disciplines is also represented: agronomists, specialists in tropical agriculture, groundwater, agricultural credit or livestock, demographers, architects, rural and urban sociologists, public health experts, environmentalists, educators, energy specialists, and physical planners. Typically, technical specialists come to the Bank in mid-career, after extensive experience in their field, sometimes as managers. Most have worked in developing countries. Projects staff are expected to have a broad

understanding of development issues and the capacity and
maturity to make sound, independent judgments. It is safe to
say that, in terms of size and national and professional
diversity, the Bank's projects staff is unique.

IDENTIFICATION

The first phase of the cycle is concerned with identifying
projects that have a high priority, that appear suitable for
Bank support, and that the Bank, the government, and the
borrower are interested in considering (see box for the
definition of a borrower). In earlier years, project
identification was done *ad hoc*, largely in response to
proposals by governments and borrowers. Over the years, the
Bank has encouraged and helped borrowing countries to
develop their own planning capabilities and has also
strengthened its own methods of project generation.
Economic and sector analyses carried out by the Bank provide
a framework for evaluating national and sectoral policies and
problems and an understanding of the development potential
of the country. They also assess a country's
"creditworthiness" for Bank or IDA lending. This analysis

provides the basis for a continuing dialogue between the Bank and a country on an appropriate development strategy, including policy and institutional changes for the economy as a whole and for its major sectors. It is then possible to identify projects that fit into and support a coherent development strategy, that meet sectoral objectives, and that both the government and the Bank consider suitable. These projects must also meet a *prima facie* test of feasibility—that technical and institutional solutions are likely to be found at costs commensurate with expected benefits.

Identifying a project that meets these requirements is not easy. Knowledge required for reaching sound judgments may be lacking. The government and other lending agencies may not share the Bank's views on development objectives or sector priorities. There may be difficult choices regarding the scope of the project (Should it start with a pilot/experimental phase or with a larger but possibly more risky investment?). Differences may quickly surface over the need for policy or institutional reforms to achieve the project's objectives. Work on resolving some of these issues may extend well into the preparation stage.

In practice, how are projects identified within this context? Both the Bank and the government are involved, making the process complex, and this complexity is compounded by the differing capabilities of governments for handling economic planning and project generation. The Bank's economic analysis of a country is affected by the extent and quality of the country's data base and its own economic work. Sector analysis might be done by the country itself, or might be carried out by the Bank or through one of the Bank's cooperative programs with a specialized UN agency, or through studies financed by the United Nations Development Programme (UNDP), bilateral aid programs, or a specific provision for studies in a previous Bank loan.

Finally, some projects are brought forward by private sponsors, such as mining and petroleum enterprises, seeking to develop new resources. These projects have to meet the standards described previously before being regarded as "identified" from the Bank's point of view.

Once identified, projects are incorporated into a multi-year lending program for each country that forms the basis for the Bank's future work in the country. Country programs are used for programming and budgeting the Bank's operations and for assuring that the resources necessary to bring each project forward through the successive phases of its cycle are available.

PREPARATION

After a project has been incorporated into the lending program, it enters the project pipeline, and an extensive period—normally one or two years—of close collaboration between the Bank and the eventual borrower begins. A "project brief" is prepared for each project, describing its objectives, identifying principal issues, and establishing the timetable for its further processing. It is difficult to generalize about the preparation phase because of the variables that abound: the nature of the project, the experience and capability of the borrower, the knowledge currently available (Is it the first loan to the sector/borrower or a "repeater"?), the sources and availability of financing for preparation, and the nature of the relationships between the Bank, the government, cofinancers, and other donors that may be involved in the sector or project.

Formal responsibility for preparation rests with the borrower. At one time, the Bank was reluctant to assist in project preparation, on the banker's principle that such involvement might prejudice its objectivity at appraisal. But experience has shown that the Bank must have an active role in ensuring a timely flow of well-prepared projects. That role has a number of aspects: making sure that borrowers with the capacity and resources to prepare projects themselves understand the Bank's requirements and standards; helping other borrowers to find the financing or technical assistance necessary for preparatory work; and filling gaps in projects that have been incompletely or inadequately prepared. There are even exceptional circumstances in which the Bank itself does preparatory work. The Bank's regional missions in Eastern and Western Africa were established primarily to supplement the limited capabilities of governments in those regions to identify and prepare sound projects.

Financial and technical assistance for project preparation can be extended in a number of ways. The Bank can provide special loans for technical assistance or detailed engineering, make advances from its Project Preparation Facility, reimburse the borrower under the loan in question for preparatory work done earlier, or include funds for preparatory work in a loan for another project in the sector. Cooperative programs between the Bank and the Food and Agriculture Organization of the United Nations (FAO), the United Nations Educational, Scientific, and Cultural Organization (Unesco), the World Health Organization (WHO), and the United Nations Industrial Development Organization (UNIDO) are also an important source of support, as are the UNDP and bilateral aid programs.

While most other assistance for project preparation is provided on a grant basis, and hence is especially attractive, Bank financing must be repaid by the borrower. In providing this help, care must be taken that the project is not perceived at this stage as "the Bank's project" and that the government and the borrower are fully committed to the project and deeply involved in its preparation. This care is more relevant to the "new-style" projects than to traditional infrastructure projects that involve well-established entities whose objectives, and ways of achieving them, are reasonably clear. In new-style projects, such conditions often do not exist, so the commitment of the government and the borrower is essential not only for preparation, but, even more, for successful implementation.

Preparation must cover the full range of technical, institutional, economic, and financial conditions necessary to achieve the project's objectives. For example, a resettlement project might require studies based on remote sensing data to locate arable land, transportation corridors, and the population living in the area proposed for resettlement. Verification on the ground would be followed by a more detailed investigation of soils and water resources; determination of appropriate cropping patterns on the basis of available resources and research knowledge; selection of the technical package necessary for increasing crop yields; and economic and sociological studies of the people being settled to determine appropriate systems of land tenure, extension services, marketing systems, project management, and other institutional arrangements. Government policies with respect to the costs of inputs and the prices of farm products would be studied, as well as levels and methods of cost recovery and their impact on the financial position of the beneficiaries and the government. The role of the private sector in relation to the project would be yet another subject to be examined.

A critical element of preparation is identifying and comparing technical and institutional alternatives for achieving the project's objectives. Most developing countries are characterized by abundant, inexpensive labor and scarce capital. The Bank, therefore, is not looking for the most advanced technological solutions, but for those that are most appropriate to the country's resource endowment and stage of development. Though the Bank has financed advanced telecommunications equipment and modern container-port facilities, project officers nevertheless must consider such questions as whether oxen are more economical than tractors for crop cultivation; whether slum upgrading or sites and services are more suitable than conventional housing as minimal accommodation for the urban poor; or whether public standpipes are more appropriate than house connections for water supply. Preparation thus requires feasibility studies that identify and prepare preliminary designs of technical and institutional alternatives, compare their respective costs and benefits, and investigate in more detail the more promising alternatives until the most satisfactory solution is finally worked out.

All this takes time, and the Bank is sometimes criticized for the length of time required to make a loan. But for the countries concerned, each project represents a major investment with a long economic life, and the time spent in arriving at the best technical solution, in setting up the proper organization, and in anticipating and dealing in advance with marketing and other problems, usually pays for itself several times over.

APPRAISAL

As the project takes shape and studies near completion, the project is scheduled for appraisal. Appraisal, perhaps the best known phase of project work (in part, because it is the culmination of preparatory work), provides a comprehensive review of all aspects of the project and lays the foundation for implementing the project and evaluating it when completed.

Appraisal is solely the Bank's responsibility. It is conducted by Bank staff, sometimes supplemented by individual consultants, who usually spend three to four weeks in the field. If preparation has been done well, appraisal can be relatively straightforward; if not, a subsequent mission, or missions, to the country may be necessary to complete the job. Appraisal covers four major aspects of the project—technical, institutional, economic, and financial.

TECHNICAL. The Bank has to ensure that projects are soundly designed, appropriately engineered, and follow accepted agronomic, educational, or other standards. The appraisal mission looks into technical alternatives considered, solutions proposed, and expected results.

More concretely, technical appraisal is concerned with questions of physical scale, layout, and location of facilities; what technology is to be used, including types of equipment or processes and their appropriateness to local conditions; what approach will be followed for the provision of services; how realistic implementation schedules are; and what the likelihood is of achieving expected levels of output. In a family planning project, the technical appraisal might be concerned with the number, design, and location of maternal and child health clinics and the appropriateness of the services offered to the needs of the population being served; in highways, with the width and pavement of the roads in relation to expected traffic and the trade-offs between initial construction costs and recurrent costs for maintenance, and between more or less labor-intensive methods of construction; in education, with whether the proposed curriculum and the number and layout of classrooms, laboratories, and other facilities are suited to the country's educational needs.

A critical part of technical appraisal is a review of the cost estimates and the engineering or other data on which they are based to determine whether they are accurate within an acceptable margin and whether allowances for physical contingencies and expected price increases during implementation are adequate. The technical appraisal also reviews proposed procurement arrangements to make sure that the Bank's requirements are met. Procedures for obtaining engineering, architectural, or other professional services are examined. In addition, technical appraisal is concerned with estimating the costs of operating project facilities and services and with the availability of necessary raw materials or other inputs. The potential impact of the project on the human and physical environment is examined to make sure that any adverse effects will be controlled or minimized.

INSTITUTIONAL. In the Bank's current terminology, "institution building" has become perhaps the most important purpose of Bank lending. This means that the transfer of financial resources and the construction of physical facilities, however valuable in their own right, are less important in the long run than the creation of a sound and viable local "institution," interpreted in its broadest sense to cover not only the borrowing entity itself, its organization, management, staffing, policies, and procedures, but also the whole array of government policies that conditions the environment in which the institution operates.

Experience indicates that insufficient attention to the institutional aspects of a project leads to problems during its implementation and operation. Institutional appraisal is concerned with a host of questions, such as whether the entity is properly organized and its management adequate to do the job, whether local capabilities and initiative are being used effectively, and whether policy or institutional changes are required outside the entity to achieve project objectives.

These questions are important for traditional project entities; they are even more important (and difficult to answer) for the entities charged with preparing and carrying out the new-style projects intended to benefit the rural and urban poor, where there may be no established institutional pattern to follow. The Bank's experience to date has not yielded any ready-made solutions for putting together an institution that can effectively and economically deliver goods and services to large numbers of people—often in remote areas and outside the ordinary ambit of government—and that can motivate them and change their behavior.

Of all the aspects of a project, institution building is perhaps the most difficult to come to grips with. In part, this is because its success depends so much on an understanding of the cultural environment. The Bank has come to recognize the need for a continuing re-examination of institutional arrangements, an openness to new ideas, and a willingness to adopt a long-term approach that may extend over several projects.

ECONOMIC. Through cost-benefit analysis of alternative project designs, the one that contributes most to the development objectives of the country may be selected. This analysis is normally done in successive stages during project preparation, but appraisal is the point at which the final review and assessment are made.

During economic appraisal, the project is studied in its sectoral setting. The investment program for the sector, the strengths and weaknesses of public and private sectoral institutions, and key government policies are all examined.

In transportation, each appraisal considers the transportation system as a whole and its contribution to the country's economic development. A highway appraisal examines the relationship with competing modes of transport such as railways. Transport policies throughout the sector are reviewed and changes recommended, for example, in any regulatory practices that distort the allocation of traffic. In education, power, and telecommunications, the "project" as defined by the Bank may embrace the investment program of the whole sector. In agriculture, which is more diversified and accounts for a much larger share of a developing country's economic activity, it is more difficult to formulate a comprehensive strategy for the sector; attention is given to sectoral issues such as land tenure, the adequacy of incentives for farmers, marketing arrangements, availability of public services, and governmental tax, pricing, and subsidy policies.

Whenever the current state of the art permits, projects are subjected to a detailed analysis of their costs and benefits to the country, the result of which is usually expressed as an economic rate of return. This analysis often requires the solution of difficult problems, such as how to determine the physical consequences of the project and how to value them in terms of the development objectives of the country.

Over the years, the Bank has kept in close touch with progress in the methodology of economic appraisal. "Shadow" prices are used routinely when true economic values of costs are not reflected in market prices as a result of various distortions, such as trade restrictions, taxes, or subsidies. These shadow price adjustments are made most frequently in the exchange rate and labor costs used in the calculations. The distribution of the benefits of a project and its fiscal impact are considered carefully, and the use of "social" prices to give proper weight in the cost-benefit analysis to the government's objectives of improved income distribution and increased public savings is passing through an experimental phase. Since the estimates of future costs and benefits are subject to substantial margins of error, an analysis is always made of the sensitivity of the return on the project to variations in some of the key assumptions.

Less frequently, in cases of major uncertainty, a risk/probability analysis is also carried out. The optimal timing of the investment is tested in relation to the first year's benefits. When the Bank provides funds to intermediate agencies (development finance companies, agricultural credit institutions) for relending to smaller operations, or in the case of sector lending, those agencies' own appraisal methods must be acceptable.

Some of the elements of project costs and benefits, such as pollution control, better health or education, or manpower training, may defy quantification; in other projects, for example electric power or telecommunications, it may be necessary to use proxies, such as revenues, that do not fully measure the value of the service to the economy. In some cases, it is possible to assess alternative solutions that have the same benefits and to select the least-cost solution. In other cases, for example education, alternatives are likely to involve different benefits as well as different costs, and a qualitative assessment must suffice.

Whether qualitative or quantitative, the economic analysis always aims at assessing the contribution of the project to the development objectives of the country; this remains the basic criterion for project selection and appraisal. And while greater concern with the distributional effects of projects reflects broader objectives of development, it does not mean that the Bank has lowered its standards of appraisal. Whether "old" style or "new," every project must have a satisfactory economic return, a standard that the Bank believes serves the best interests of both the country and the Bank itself.

FINANCIAL. Financial appraisal has several purposes. One is to ensure that there are sufficient funds to cover the costs of implementing the project. The Bank does not normally lend for all project costs; typically, it finances foreign exchange costs and expects the borrower or the government to meet some or all of the local costs. In addition, other cofinancers, such as the European Development Fund, the several Arab funds, the regional development banks, bilateral aid agencies, and a growing number of commercial banks, are joining to an increasing extent in cofinancing projects that, in many instances, are appraised and supervised by the Bank. Therefore, an important aspect of appraisal is to ensure that there is a financing plan that will make funds available to implement the project on schedule. When funds are to be provided by a government known to have difficulty in raising local revenues, special arrangements may be proposed, such as advance appropriations to a revolving fund or the earmarking of tax proceeds.

For a revenue-producing enterprise, financial appraisal is also concerned with financial viability. Will it be able to meet all its financial obligations, including debt service to the Bank? Will it be able to generate enough funds from internal resources to earn a reasonable rate of return on its assets and make a satisfactory contribution to its future capital requirements? The finances of the enterprise are closely reviewed through projections of the balance sheet, income statement, and cash flow. Where financial accounts are inadequate, a new accounting system may be established with technical assistance financed out of the loan. Additional safeguards of financial integrity may include establishing suitable debt-to-equity ratios or limitations on additional long-term borrowing.

The financial review often highlights the need to adjust the level and structure of prices charged by the enterprise. Whether or not they are publicly owned, enterprises assisted by the Bank generally provide basic services and come under close public scrutiny. Because the government may wish to subsidize such services to the consuming public as a matter of policy, or perhaps simply as the line of least resistance, it may be reluctant to approve the price increases necessary to ensure efficient use of the output of the enterprise and to meet its financial objectives. But adequate prices are a *sine qua non* of Bank lending to revenue-earning enterprises, and the question of rate adjustments may be critical to the appraisal and subsequent implementation of a project.

Financial appraisal is also concerned with recovering investment and operating costs from project beneficiaries. The Bank normally expects farmers to pay, over time and out of their increased production, all of the operating costs and at least a substantial part of the capital costs of, say, an irrigation project. Actual recovery in each case takes account of the income position of the beneficiaries and of practical problems such as the difficulties of administering a particular system of charges or of levying higher charges on Bank-assisted projects than are collected elsewhere. The Bank's policy thus tries to strike a balance between considerations of equity, the need to use scarce resources efficiently, and the need to generate additional funds to replicate the project and reach larger numbers of potential beneficiaries.

Costs can be recovered in a variety of ways—by charges for irrigation water, through general taxation, or by requiring farmers to sell their crops to a government marketing agency at controlled prices. Some countries apply lower standards of cost recovery than those recommended by the Bank; thus, arriving at a common judgment on what is desirable and practicable can be one of the more difficult aspects of the appraisal and subsequent negotiation.

To ensure the efficient use of scarce capital, the Bank believes that interest charges to the ultimate beneficiaries should generally reflect the opportunity cost of money in the economy (indicating the cost of foregone alternatives). But interest rates are often subsidized, and the rate of inflation may even exceed the interest rate. In countries with high rates of inflation, a system of indexed rates is sometimes followed. As in the case of cost recovery, the appropriate level of interest rates may be a contentious issue. The Bank may have to set its sights on a long-term goal, recognizing that it will take time to bring about what may be far-reaching changes in financial policy. This may be particularly so when the government is seeking to control interest rates and other prices as part of an anti-inflation program.

The appraisal mission prepares a report that sets forth its findings and recommends terms and conditions of the loan. This report is drafted and redrafted and carefully reviewed before the loan is approved by the management of the Bank for negotiations with the borrower. Because of the Bank's close involvement in identification and preparation, appraisal rarely results in rejection of a project; but it may be extensively modified or redesigned during this process to correct flaws that otherwise might have led to its rejection.

NEGOTIATIONS, BOARD PRESENTATION

Negotiation is the stage at which the Bank and the borrower endeavor to agree on the measures necessary to assure the success of the project. These agreements are then converted into legal obligations, set out in the loan documents. The Bank may have agreed with a public utility borrower that, to earn an adequate rate of return and finance a reasonable proportion of its investments, prices are to be increased by, say, 20 percent immediately and 10 percent in two years' time. A financial covenant to be agreed upon during negotiation will define the overall financial objectives and specify the necessary rate of return and the timing of the initial rate increase. If a new project unit must be set up to administer the project or to coordinate the activities of the various ministries involved, the loan documents will specify when and how it is to be established and staffed. In fact, all of the principal issues that have been raised prior to and during appraisal are dealt with in the loan documents. Thus, the drafting and negotiation of the legal documents are an essential part of the process of ensuring that the borrower and the Bank are in agreement, not only on the broad objectives of the project, but also on the specific actions necessary to achieve them and the detailed schedule for project implementation.

Negotiations are a process of give and take on both sides of the table. The Bank, for its part, must learn to adapt its general policies to what can reasonably be accomplished in the country, the sector, and the particular setting of the project. The borrower, for its part, must recognize that the Bank's advice is generally based on professional expertise and worldwide experience, and that the Bank's requirement that its funds be invested wisely is compatible with the best interests of the project. Despite differences that inevitably arise when difficult issues must be resolved, the relations that have developed over time between the Bank and its borrowers at this and other stages of the project cycle are generally very good. Bank staff have become more aware of, and sensitive to, local conditions that are critical to the success of a project. Borrowers have come to appreciate that the Bank's approach is professional and objective, that it is in business to lend for well-conceived and well-executed projects, and that this is indeed the Bank's only interest in project work.

After negotiations, the appraisal report, amended to reflect the agreements reached, together with the President's report and the loan documents, is presented to the Bank's Executive Directors. If the Executive Directors approve the operation, the loan is then signed in a simple ceremony that marks the end of one stage of the cycle and the beginning of another.

IMPLEMENTATION AND SUPERVISION

The next stage in the life of a project is its actual implementation over the period of construction and subsequent operation. Implementation, of course, is the responsibility of the borrower, with whatever assistance has been agreed upon with the Bank in such forms as organizational studies, training of staff, expatriate managers, or consultants to help supervise construction. The Bank's role is to supervise the project as it is implemented.

Supervision is the least glamorous part of project work, but in several respects it is the most important. Once the loan for a particular project is signed, attention in the borrowing country shifts to new projects that are coming along; this attitude is understandable and it is reinforced by the fact that many months or years may elapse before the "old" project begins to yield tangible results. Nevertheless, it is obvious that no matter how well a project has been identified, prepared, and appraised, its development benefits can be realized only when it has been properly executed. All projects face implementation problems, some of which cannot be foreseen. These problems may stem from difficulties inherent in the development process or from more specific causes such as changes in the economic and political situation, in project management, or even in the weather. As a result, although the development objectives of a project generally remain constant, its implementation path often varies from that which was envisaged.

It is for these reasons that the Bank has decided that adequate supervision should be the first priority in the assignment of project staff. In practice, the resources devoted to supervision have increased substantially over the years, both absolutely and relative to other project tasks.

The Bank is required by its Articles of Agreement to make arrangements to "ensure that the proceeds of any loan are used only for the purposes for which the loan was granted." While this "watchdog" function has been and remains important, the main purpose of supervision is to help ensure that projects achieve their development objectives and, in particular, to work with the borrowers in identifying and dealing with problems that arise during implementation. Supervision, therefore, is primarily an exercise in collective problem solving, and, as such, is one of the most effective ways in which the Bank provides technical assistance to its member countries.

Over the years another central objective of supervision has emerged: gathering the accumulated experience to "feed back" into the design and preparation of future projects and into the improvement of policies and procedures. Monitoring and evaluation units are now frequently incorporated, particularly in the new-style projects, to gather information for this purpose. An annual review of the supervision portfolio as a whole is conducted to identify major issues of implementation and recommend appropriate changes in Bank policies and procedures.

Supervision takes place in a variety of ways. During negotiation, agreement will have been reached on a schedule of progress reports to be submitted by the borrower. These reports cover the physical execution of the project, its costs, the financial status of revenue-earning enterprises, and information on the evolution of project benefits.

Progress reports are reviewed at headquarters. Problems that surface are dealt with by correspondence or in the course of the field missions that are sent to every project. The frequency of these missions is closely tailored to the complexity of the project, the status of its implementation, and the number and nature of problems encountered. In the periodic internal reviews of projects under supervision, currently numbering about 1,600, some projects are classified as belonging to a special "problem" category. These projects, usually about 10 percent of the total, are watched with particular care and may be visited three or four times a year.

An important element of project supervision concerns procurement of goods and works financed under the loan. Procurement is carried out in accordance with guidelines, incorporated into every loan agreement, that are designed to ensure that the requisite goods and works are procured in the most efficient and economical manner. In most cases, this objective can best be achieved through international competitive bidding open to qualified contractors or manufacturers from all of the Bank's member countries and Switzerland and Taiwan, China. To foster the development of local capabilities, a degree of preference is accorded to domestic suppliers and, under certain conditions, to domestic contractors. Local competitive bidding, or even construction by the borrower's own forces, may be more economic and efficient in some projects for which the works are too small for international tendering to be appropriate.

Seeing that the agreed-upon procurement rules are observed in practice—a single loan may involve anywhere from a few individual contracts to several hundred—is a time-consuming job and one that the Bank takes very seriously. Sometimes the job is relatively straightforward and routine; on other occasions, major issues arise, as, for example, in a telecommunications or power project when there may be a very close choice among several international suppliers as to which has made the lowest evaluated bid on a multimillion dollar contract. The borrower, not the Bank, is responsible for preparing the specifications and tender documents and evaluating bids. The Bank's role is to make sure that the borrower's work is done properly and the guidelines are observed so that Bank funds may be disbursed for the contract. Any controversy concerning the proposed award is sure to be called promptly to the Bank's attention.

Consultant services in such fields as economics, management, finance, architecture, and engineering also must be contracted for by borrowers. Because the quality of these services is usually of overriding importance and can vary widely among firms, consideration of price, as applied to goods and works, is normally not appropriate, although it may be used in special circumstances. With respect to such contracting by borrowers, the Bank's role—as outlined in recently published guidelines—is to ensure that the firms considered for selection are treated equitably and that the firm selected is able to provide services of appropriate quality. For this work, too, the Bank encourages consideration of qualified firms from the borrowing country—either alone or in joint ventures—as well as firms from other developing countries.

EVALUATION

While supervision is, in part, a process of learning through experience, it is primarily concerned with that period in the project's life when physical components are being constructed, equipment purchased and installed, and new institutions, programs, and policies put in place. Once these stages are complete, and Bank funds fully disbursed, the level of supervision declines sharply. During the period of active supervision, attention tends to be focused on the problems of the moment. While projects may be subject to ongoing monitoring and evaluation, the need for a more comprehensive approach to evaluating project results has become apparent. In 1970, an evaluation system was established as the final stage in the project cycle.

All Bank-assisted projects are now subject to an *ex post* audit. To ensure its independence and objectivity, this audit is the responsibility of the Operations Evaluation Department (OED), which is entirely separate from the operating staff of the Bank and which reports directly to the Executive Directors. While this system ensures full accountability, it is also designed to mesh closely with, and take advantage of, the supervision activity of the operating staff.

As the final step in supervision, regular projects staff—or the borrower—prepare a completion report on each project at the end of the disbursement period. These reports are, in part, an exercise in self-evaluation—which has not prevented them from being frank and often critical. Each report is reviewed by the OED, which then prepares a separate audit report; both reports are sent to the Executive Directors. Most audits are based on a desk review of all materials pertaining to the project, but, whenever necessary, the audit staff undertakes a field review, sometimes as comprehensive as the original appraisal. Borrowers are asked to comment on the OED audits and are requested to prepare their own completion reports. Furthermore, the Bank encourages borrowers to establish evaluation systems to review all their development investments.

Each audit and completion report re-estimates the economic rate of return on the basis of actual implementation costs and updated information on operating costs and expected benefits. It cannot, however, pass a final judgment on the success or failure of some projects whose economic lives, with their attendant operating costs and benefits, extend well beyond the end of the disbursement period. To meet this need, OED prepares "impact evaluation reports" at least five years after the last disbursement for a small number of carefully selected projects. Borrowers play an active role in this process, too.

In addition, an annual OED report reviews all project audits. Studies are made in greater depth of groups of projects (such as all loans to development finance companies), special problems (such as delays in loan effectiveness), or a sector in a particular country (such as agricultural projects in Indonesia).

The evaluation system is a gold mine of information, supplementing and complementing that provided by the broader stream of project supervision reports. Some of the findings are sobering; many are reassuring. Experience indicates, for example, that the Bank still has much to learn about technologies necessary to bring about sustained increases in yields of small farmers in rainfed areas, most notably in sub-Saharan Africa. Problems of cost overruns and delayed completion have plagued the implementation of a number of projects, particularly in the period following the oil price rises and ensuing worldwide inflation. Many projects change in scope during their implementation. Nevertheless, the most recent* annual review of the OED audits, comprising eighty-seven projects, indicates that over 93 percent of the investments remain worthwhile, and that a number of them had expected economic returns better than those estimated at appraisal.

Particularly gratifying is the indication that the Bank's response to the lessons of experience is generally positive. Mistakes, of which the Bank has had its share, are not often repeated. Subsequent projects build on earlier ones in the same sector. New approaches, policies, and procedures have been adopted to improve project performance: For example, the project brief system is helping to secure government agreement and commitment to project objectives at an earlier stage of project design; rural development projects now integrate the provision of all the services, inputs, and basic infrastructure necessary to bring about a sustained increase in small farmers' yields; lending for projects that are at a more advanced stage of preparation is being introduced to provide more accurate cost estimates and reduce the likelihood of cost overruns and implementation delays.

The lessons of experience are thus being built into the design and preparation of future projects. In other words, the project cycle is working as intended.

---

*Seventh Annual Review of Project Performance Audit Results. (Washington: World Bank). December 1981.

PROJECT PREPARATION HANDBOOK

VOLUME 1: GUIDELINES

PROJECT DATA SHEET AND GUIDELINES

.

GWS/81.3
ORIGINAL: ENGLISH

INTERNATIONAL DRINKING WATER SUPPLY AND SANITATION DECADE
PROJECT DATA SHEET

1981-1990

For further information see the booklet: Project and Programme Information System, WHO March 1981 and the Project Preparation Handbook for the Water Supply and Sanitation Sector issued by the World Bank.

---

1. COUNTRY: 2. <u>No</u>.

---

3. <u>TITLE</u>:

---

4. TYPE OF PROJECT AND SCOPE:

---

5. BACKGROUND AND OBJECTIVE:

---

6. RESPONSIBLE GOVERNMENT AGENCY:

---

7. INSTITUTIONAL SUPPORT:

---

8. DURATION: 9. STARTING DATE:

GWS/81.2
page 2

10. SUMMARY OF ESTIMATED PROJECT COSTS:

    Foreign   Local   Total

11. TENTATIVE FINANCING PLAN:

    (i) Requirements   (ii) Sources

12. FINANCIAL STRATEGY:

13. SECTOR DEVELOPMENT PERFORMANCE:

14. OUTPUTS:

15. GOVERNMENT PRIORITY AND COMMITTMENT:

16. EXPECTED BENEFITS:

17. PREPARED BY: DATE:

GWS/81.2
page 3

GUIDELINES TO COMPLETE PROJECT DATA SHEET

1. <u>Country</u>   Name of country. State also region where project is implemented.

2. <u>No.</u>   Data sheets will be numbered sequentially for each country as projects are identified and data sheets prepared.

3. <u>Title</u>   State full title of project.

4. <u>Type of Project and Scope</u>   State briefly the type of project concerned and the scope of activities, e.g. investment - pre-investment project, financial analysis, tariff study, institutional study, master planning, operational assistance, technical design, manpower development, legal instruments improvement, research and development, public information, relief and emergency, community participation, quality surveillance and control, local manufacturing and logistics etc.

5. <u>Background and Objective</u>   (i) Indicate how the project fits into the country's development programme and its linkage to the sector. In this connection indicate what the project adds to the country, the economy and the sector.

(ii) Describe relation of project to other externally assisted projects. State year of start or completion and status of these projects. Indicate donors and external agencies assisting the sector.

(iii) Indicate if there is community participation and involvement envisaged in project implementation.

(iv) State and describe existing studies (indicating title and year), as well as date, information etc. available relevant to the project.

6. <u>Responsible Government Agency</u>   Indicate exact name and address of Government agency responsible for the implementation of the project and to which correspondence should be directed.

7. <u>Institutional Support</u>   (i) Describe existing and expected support for operation and maintenance of systems. Also indicate whether funds have been earmarked for operation and maintenance of systems once they are built.

(ii) State if project will operate on cost recovery basis. If not, indicate who will pay for the recurrent costs and to what extent.

(iii) Indicate the type of organization and management is available for project implementation.

8. <u>Duration</u>   Expected duration of project. Duration of each phase if applicable.

9. <u>Starting Date</u>   Tentative timing for the start of the project. Also indicate what actions will indicate the start of the project.

10. <u>Summary of Estimated Project Costs</u>   Estimate total costs in US dollars for the project and for each major project component. Indicate proportions of component and total costs to come from foreign and from local sources. If project is a pre-investment or direct support project rather than an investment project, indicate the following:

    Local Inputs   (i) Personnel: State number and designation of counterpart national staff assigned to project. Indicate if possible, their background, experience etc. and the support they can provide to project.

GWS/81.2   page 4

(ii) Equipment and supplies: Indicate vehicles, equipment etc. allotted to project.

(iii) Funds: Specify Government contribution to project, in cash and kind in US dollars.

Foreign Inputs   (i) Personnel: State number, background and field of expertise required of foreign experts, consultants etc with man months in each case.

(ii) Equipment and supplies: Indicate if any equipment and supplies are to be provided from external sources.

(iii) Funds: State amount of external funding required in US dollars.

11. Tentative Financing Plan   (only for investment projects)

(i) Requirements: The total financing required for the project, comprised of the total estimated project cost and the working capital needed.

(ii) Sources: Indicate sources of the total financing required, from sector agencies responsible for the project, from external agencies and from the Government.

12. Financial Strategy   (only for investment projects)

(i) Describe plans and a timetable for meeting operating, maintenance and debt service expenses of the project once it is completed.

13. Sector Development Performance   (i) Indicate and name how many similar or related projects have been implemented.

(ii) State what Government support has been given to sector development.

14. Outputs   (i) State the nature of studies that will come out of the project. Also improvement in the institutional aspects etc.

15. Government Priority and Committment   (i) Indicate if project is included in Government development plan and country programme.

(ii) Indicate degree of Government priority and committment to project.

16. Expected Benefits   (i) Indicate total population that will be served as a result of the project. Also what groups will be the beneficiaries (type of consumer, hospitals, industry etc.)

(ii) Indicate expected improvement in health and socioeconomic conditions.

(iii) Indicate personnel (number, types etc) expected to be trained as a result of project and improvement in local sector manpower situation.

17. Prepared by   State name of official who completed the data sheet or provided the relevant data for its completion.

=   =   =